Sacred Smoke

The Magic and Medicine of Palo Santo

David Crow

Published by Floracopeia Aromatic Treasures

FLORACOPEIA
AROMATIC·TREASURES

Copyright © 2012 David Crow

This book is intended as an educational reference guide only, not a medical manual. The information given here is designed to help make informed decisions about your health. It is not intended as a substitute for any treatment that may have been prescribed by your medical professional. The author takes no responsibility for the misinterpretation and deliberate or accidental misuse of the information presented in this book, or on the websites.

www.floracopeia.com

Dedication

This book is dedicated to Dante and Rocio, with love, from David and Sara.

Acknowledgements

This little book would not have been possible without the kindness and support of several people. Many thanks to everyone at Floracopeia for giving me the time, freedom and encouragement to make this journey and then write about it: Jai Dev Singh, Darren Engstrom, Taya Malakian, Wendy Johnson, Ricardo Rico and Meghan Archer.

Much gratitude also goes to the people along the way who played small and large roles in weaving together the entire chain of events: Sarada Von Sonn, Robert Svoboda, Eric Horstman, and James Peterson. Many thanks to Eric Horstman for writing the preface.

Special thanks are due to Mojohito Richerson von Tchudi for his many hours of work preparing this text for publication, and to Jai Dev Singh and Ricardo Rico for their assistance with launching it.

A very special thank you goes to my father, Dr. James Crow, who diligently proofread the manuscript and offered many astute editorial comments.

The greatest thanks are due to Dante Bolcato, for his twelve years of dedicated work, his ongoing production of a deeply healing aromatic medicine, his wisdom, humor, and generosity. Thanks also to Rocio, his love, for opening their home for our visit.

Many thanks to all the people who carry on the important work at El Artesan, most of whom I do not know by name, but especially to Lazaro, Lilliana, Lucio, and Barbara Bolcato.

Finally, my deepest gratitude and appreciation goes to my wife, Sara Crow, for documenting this adventure and providing the photographs for this book, for patiently tolerating the hardships of the journey, and for her continual love and support.

Table of Contents

Foreword

Ecuador is one of a small group of "megadiverse" countries that among them harbor up to 65 percent of all the world's species. Among its many tree species is the enigmatic Palo Santo, which I first met in the late 1980's in the Galapagos Islands. I would often see the distinct gray-barked trees in the lowlands of Santa Cruz Island, but I never imagined their incredible story.

In the early 1990's when I returned to Ecuador as a Peace Corps volunteer to work in Cerro Blanco, one of the last remaining large tracts of dry tropical forest remaining on the Ecuadorian coast, I would smell the pungent Palo Santo smoke wafting into the open window of my car as I passed through neighborhoods of Guayaquil, where it was used as a natural insect repellant against the hordes of mosquitoes that appeared in the rainy season.

My later work as Director of the Pro-Forest Foundation again brought me into contact with Palo Santo, as we incorporated it into a long-term dry tropical forest restoration program. We have never been able to grow large numbers of the Palo Santo, because the preferred propagation method of seed collection often ends in failure, as birds quickly gobble the tasty red seeds before they have fully ripened.

"*Sacred Smoke*" chronicles the love affair of one man, Dante Bolcato (El Maestro), with Palo Santo. It is the story of his efforts to raise awareness of the deep medicinal and therapeutic powers of this tree and share them with both Ecuadorians and people throughout the world through innovative companies like Floracopeia and its visionary founder, David Crow.

Ecuador is at a crossroads. With one of the highest deforestation rates in South America, much of its native forest has been cut down and converted into cattle pastures and agricultural land to feed a growing population that is expanding into towns and cities. At the same time, Ecuador is the first country to recognize the rights of nature in its national constitution.

To help insure the future of Ecuador's stunning natural heritage, we need people like Dante Bolcato and fair trade initiatives such as that spearheaded by David Crow to preserve the Palo Santo tree and the critically endangered Ecuadorian dry tropical forest through the sustainable harvesting of products that provide tangible benefits to local people. I hope that the work of Dante and David continue to flourish and grow.

Eric Horstman *has worked for the last twenty years in protected-area management and biodiversity conservation focusing on dry tropical forests in Ecuador. He lives with his family at the Cerro Blanco Protected Forest on the outskirts of Guayaquil.*

www.bosquecerroblanco.org

I

Into the Fire

An auspicious wind is blowing off the Bay of Bengal, carrying warm marine fragrances through the night sky. The temples of Mahabalipuram stand silently on Tamil Nadu's dark horizon, as the flames of a small fire dance before us.

What is this auspiciousness that graces the air?

Sometimes a small event leads to something great, a tiny gesture creates an unexpected series of fortunate consequences that could never be predicted at the time, but seen only in retrospect. In retrospect, one might sense that such an event was the opening play of an irresistible destiny about to unfold, as if an invisible presence had already cast the players of the story and would now gently touch their lives, beckoning. A small event of this type is about to happen.

Threads of auspicious events have brought me here to the southeastern coast of India. I came from Taiwan, where I had been staying with the Dharma Master Hsin Tao at his mountain monastery, living as a guest in a small room where the rain and wind howled at night and pristine ocean views stretched away across the eastern Pacific when the sun came out. When Hsin Tao set off on a pilgrimage to his native Burma I accompanied him and after returning to Taipei by way of Rangoon, proceeded to Chennai.

The circle of people seated in the sand is auspicious as well, and the purpose and reason for their being here. We are devotees of Ayurveda, gathered at a beachside resort for a conference devoted to this ancient medical art and science. A few Western teachers have been invited to speak to the Indian students, eager to hear of the possibilities their own traditions may hold for them as a career, as a source of respect, as a way of serving, as a path to knowledge. A tiny minority of Western students, most of them now seated just out of reach of the flames, are here to learn from the Indian doctors who are sharing their methods and wisdom.

I was not among the speakers at this conference, but had come to listen to those I consider my mentors and friends. To those outside the world of Ayurveda their names would mean little, except for Deepak Chopra: a casually elegant figure of mythical charisma dressed in black, who spent the day sharing a rare genius that bent the mind back and forth between micro- and macrocosms, Vedic Seers and quantum physics, dazzling the young students with visions of hope that some day Ayurveda might be elevated to a higher status of greater respect and prosperous livelihood. To those familiar with the teachers of Ayurveda in the West, our little circle around the fire would be considered a gathering of humble yet accomplished luminaries.

There is one member of this group who is about to play a lead role in the unfolding of this story. Outwardly, he is a scholar, a teacher and a writer; tonight he is his true self, a Tantric yogi. He has invited us to join him on the beach to build this fire, and, as is his habit, custom and practice, to worship. And so we are worshipping, in an easygoing and relaxed way that could be expected of such a group in such a place, the Tantric leading us in chanting, singing and reciting mantras, throwing handfuls of rice, spices, resins, woods, and other savory offerings into the delighted blazing presence of the sun and its life-giving powers before us as one form of divinity after another is honored.

The tale begins at this moment, the first step of the journey is imminent; little do I know that it will take me around the world twice and back to this same fire.

The Tantric takes out a small piece of yellow wood from his cloth bag of mysteries and shaman's treasures. It falls into the fire accompanied by another chant, our voices rising and falling as the waves and wind rise and fall around us, the flames bending and stretching in the gusts. Inside those flames, embraced by the coals it has landed on, the wood undergoes a timeless alchemy.

Years of life coursing through the tree's sap, the coming and going of rainy seasons and oppressive tropical heat concentrated in its heartwood, the taste of the coastal soil flowing up its roots, the equatorial moon teasing its leaves: all these are suddenly released as perfume, blowing in spirals out of the crackling bed of the altar.

A stream of fragrance flows through space, approaching my nostrils. Was it sentient? Was intelligence guiding the way its serpentine course made its way toward my inhalation? In retrospect I would say yes, and more.

Cognizant to some degree of the phenomenon that is arising, I notice that the smoke has entered my sinuses, where the molecular presence of the tree's life work now dances into waiting receptor sites, which in turn effortlessly and with no need for self-conscious reflection, transform the entire multitude of aromatic compounds into nerve currents. Suddenly, I smell a remarkable odor, never before enjoyed, something with unmistakable notes of mystery, history, sacrament, and transcendence.

"What is that?" I ask the Tantric.

"Palo Santo," he replies.

"Where is it from?"

"It comes from South America. It is the most important fragrant tree for incense and ceremony."

"Is anyone distilling the oil?"

"Not that I know of," the yogi replies. "Maybe you should do it."

II

Botanical Intelligence

Guayaquil is hot, humid and crowded, its noisy streets full of diesel fumes and the restless spirit of poverty. Nine months have passed since the evening on the beach of Mahabalipuram.

Although I am still not aware of its presence, the sentience that is slowly spinning a web of synchronicities has something it wants me to meet here in Ecuador. It is working with a large palette of rich ingredients: a mandala of equatorial sounds and smells, people seasoned by the intensity of the environment, and the secret powers of plants from jungles, mountains and coasts.

I am here at the invitation of Eric Horstman, a man who has committed himself to the formidable task of protecting one of the country's largest remaining tropical dry forests and its disappearing flora and fauna from the encroachment of Guayaquil, a city of millions of humans needing food, water and fuel every day.

For Eric, protecting the forest is a spiritual practice, a daily discipline, a lifestyle. The forest and its inhabitants are his solace and refuge, his meditation, his source of regeneration, the oracle that provides insights to the complex challenges of his work. He walks in the forest every day and knows each tree, flower, and animal; he sees rare things of great beauty that most humans no longer have the good fortune to encounter.

Eric has been inspired by my book and the vision it articulates, a vision of the world as a garden of healing plants, a paradisiacal realm that reflects the potential of humanity's spiritual maturity. I have accepted his gracious invitation to come visit his mountain preserve of Cerro Blanco, to share with his circle of friends and colleagues the vision of a future that we both see in our mind's eye, and in return learn about the courageous battles that he is fighting to save a tiny remnant of this vision on earth.

In retrospect, it would appear that the same sentience that moved the hand of the Tantric to throw the Palo Santo wood into the fire and then blow its aromatic smoke in my direction was also what moved Eric to pick up my book and then send me his message of solidarity and hospitality. It was certainly what moved the hand of the next person in the tale.

Palo Santo is not on my mind as the congested streets of Guayaquil unfold before my fatigued eyes; I am looking forward to a massage. Eric has sent a friend to greet me at the airport, an American ex-pat chiropractor who, along with his beautiful young Latina wife, adjusts the spines and massages the muscles and stretches the joints of a dignified clientele, including the mayor of this festive, toxic, struggling, joyful, dangerous sweltering city. They take me home and put me on their tables and work out the fatigue and stress of flying from Los Angeles, sensations of tension being pulverized into submission blending with their stories of adventures with jungle tribes.

Afterwards, as I emerge from the steam room

in a pleasant euphoria, I ask if they have heard of Palo Santo.

"Everyone knows Palo Santo," the doctor replies. "It's available on every street corner. People burn it to keep mosquitoes out of the house."

"Do you know anyone distilling the oil?" I ask.

"Well, I just got a sample a couple days ago from a guy up north who is starting a project."

He returns with a small vial. Its fragrance is unique, clear and strong, fresh, full of indescribable bouquets of citruses and complex woods and deep resins and what I would later learn was a high content of limonene.

Was there an intelligence at work in the timing of this meeting between myself, the doctor, and a small vial of oil delivered by an unknown person a few days earlier? In retrospect I would say yes, and more.

III

Dante

I am driving with Eric and Don Perfecto Yagual along the coast highway to the fishing village of Puerto Lopez. We are on the way to meet Dante, an Italian who speaks no English and little Spanish;

from what I have been able to learn he is the distiller of the Palo Santo oil that has come into my hands through what is now increasingly obvious synchronicity.

Before our departure from Guayaquil I had spent time with Eric and his chief warden in the forest, hiking up rugged trails in brain-numbing heat in hopes of catching a glimpse of the rare creatures that dwell there.

Don Perfecto set the pace; although he was almost twice our age, we lagged behind, panting and drenched in sweat. He was at home among the ancient trees and tangled vines and expansive vistas and the treasures and dangers they hid, having grown up working hard in a landscape that has since mostly disappeared. Jaguars were still there, and deer and wild boars and rodents large and small and snakes and venomous insects, but it was the poachers and tree cutters that were to be feared, who stalked their precious prey in gangs, armed and ready to defend themselves.

I mention these excursions because I believe it was on such a hike that I had my first encounter with Palo Santo. It was on a long steep incline of tumbled loose stone, exposed to the tropical sun.

Don Perfecto waited ahead and as we caught up, pointed out a huge fallen tree that lay against the side of the mountain. He called it Palo Santo, and Eric agreed; he chopped a piece of the trunk with his machete and gave it to me to smell. Its fragrance was faint, compared to the piece that the Tantric had thrown in the fire on the beach in India, but similar. It had a yellowish tinge but was not the deep color I had seen before. I had assumed that it was indeed the tree, but now I was not certain; there are many things to learn when it comes to plants, and local common names are unreliable.

Dante is not there when we arrive. We peer in the window of his small shop on the beachfront street, where he sells simple handicrafts fashioned from the Palo Santo wood. An hour later than our appointed time, he arrives.

I am most curious about this Italian, and he seems equally so about me. He appears to be in his fifties, with a youthful vitality. He is short, almost gnome-like, with facial features revealing an intensely intelligent man. He is showing signs of aging, but still handsome. His gaze is penetrating, but he is easygoing.

And what is he doing here, in this tiny village

where the locals earn a bare subsistence from fishing and a little more from the seasonal hordes of Ecuadorian tourists and intoxicated youth that crowd the cafes?

It doesn't take long to glimpse the outline of Dante's story. He had been a psychotherapist, he says, with a large practice in Italy, working with families. He had a special ability to help people, especially with addictions, he claims, and I am left wondering if he possesses either some type of psychic power or was adept at hypnosis. The brightness of his eyes is intriguing, and the way they move around, so I would not have been surprised if it was true.

He cured many people, he goes on, but he could not cure himself. He was miserable, sick and exhausted. He left his practice and moved to this small village to live the last of his days as best as he could.

Then he met the Palo Santo tree.

His eyes grow brighter.

The tree saved his life, he says.

Here in Ecuador, he explains, Palo Santo is sacred, holy, mysterious and powerful. It is the healer that the people go to when all doctors and medicines have failed. They go directly to the tree, they pray to it, they ask it to cure them. The tree heals them.

He has learned many things about the tree, he continues, many things that botanists do not know: how the male and the female trees grow in families, one male among eight females; where they came from; how long they live; what happens when they die.

And the oil, I inquire?

Dante presents a liter of the liquid, in an unmarked amber bottle. I open it, and marvel that I have found an exquisite aromatic treasure hiding in a small shop on a dusty street of a tiny South American village directly on the equator.

He has only recently starting distilling, he explains, but is now producing more.

I tell him that I would like to share his excellent product with the world, and he is pleased with the idea.

But what about the sustainability of the tree, I ask, knowing that the species has been seriously overharvested.

The doctor's enthusiasm increases. He knows all about this problem, he replies. He and his assistants never cut any wood; they only walk in the forest and pick up dead branches that have fallen; the oil is superior because it has aged this way.

I am impressed. Not only are there no ethical dilemmas to resolve, it is clearly a uniquely sustainable industry.

"Come to my laboratory," the alchemist says.

IV

The Distillery

We follow Dante through the village along rutted dirt roads, into a neighborhood on the outskirts of town where the homes have more land, more space, more greenery, less open sewage.

The doctor owns the side of a hill, which he is transforming into a gigantic sculpture. Walkways wind through courtyards, courtyards sit among small cottages, cottages are adorned with gardens, gardens are layered on terraces, terraces curve along the contours of the hill. In the center of this asymmetrical mandalic landscape rises a structure that looks like a hybrid between a tipi and a conch shell, part cone, part spiral. Partly adobe, partly glass, partly tree trunks, this is his home, his castle, his dream of a new life, adorned with a spectacular view of the ocean below.

Dante invites us through the gate of his kingdom and leads us to the first large terrace where we enter a compound of small cottages, their mud walls inlaid with simple mosaics, cooled by earthen floor and green thatch overhead. Two young men are working, artisans creating products that will be sold in the store; one is chipping Palo Santo wood for incense, another is carving ornate animal figures into a huge scented candle. Dante tells us they are members of the NGO that he has created to employ members of the community, as work is scarce and the poverty is deep.

The alchemist opens the door to his distillery. It is the essence of simplicity, containing nothing but a small still with a gas burner. The red earth floor and walls are offset with turquoise window frames. It is so small that Dante stands alone inside, as we peer in.

The still came from Italy, Dante tells us. Its shape is somewhat reminiscent of old alembics, with an interesting conical lid and curved condensing tube. It arouses my curiosity, because it cannot produce any significant amount of oil, being so small.

Besides the still, the most important feature seems to be some Tarot cards, which are pasted on the walls in a pattern obvious only to the Master. They represent the fire, and alchemy and purification, he says, although I fail to understand his interpretation of the symbolism.

"I begin each distillation on the new moon," Dante says. "I distill every day for the entire lunar month. In that way I am able to get a volume of oil."

He looks at me, and I know that he knows that I know the implications of his words: how mysteries are revealed to those who contemplate the elements and their transmutations.

Seeing my comprehension, he reveals more.

"The oil changes every day. It is different in each lunar cycle. The quality and quantity are also affected by the tides."

I am definitely, and obviously, intrigued; he, in turn, appreciates this.

"A few months ago we had a series of earthquakes here," he says. "The oil changed during that time also, and more came out of the wood."

V

Emissary

I am driving back to Guayaquil with Eric and Don Perfecto, into an approaching dusk with the ocean on our right. Our visit with Dante had ended abruptly, but it had to be that way: Eric was a man with many responsibilities, and just taking a full day to bring me to Puerto Lopez was a minor miracle and an expression of immense generosity. But enough had happened already to set many future events into motion, events that I would come to see as expressions of an intelligence emanating from a tree of great power.

I was now less certain that I had actually met the Palo Santo. We did not have time to go into the forest where Dante and his team gathered the fallen branches for carving and distilling. The wood that I had seen at his home, however, was distinctly different in appearance, texture, color and odor than what I had met at Cerro Blanco, the protected forest on the edge of Guayaquil.

I was certain, however, that the liter of oil I had met in Dante's shop would soon be in the U.S. After the fascinating and tantalizing introduction to his alchemical work, we had moved from the distillery to his home, where I told him of my interest in collaborating to bring the treasure to North America. He was as intrigued with the magic of my web site as I with his distillation, and we had agreed to start working together. Although Dante was already selling small quantities of the oil locally, I was his first international customer.

It would prove to be a long and deeply rewarding relationship, not just with Dante, but also with the oil that he would gradually perfect. It would be a relationship that would begin to touch more and more people as the oil began to flow in increasing quantities from the alchemist's little still, through my little business and into the lives of those who would be touched by its fragrance, healed by its medicinal qualities, and blessed by its magic.

For me, it would also be a long and deeply rewarding relationship with the Palo Santo tree itself. I would come to understand that while my interest in this aromatic species had brought me this far and would eventually take me much farther than I could presently imagine, it was only one of the causative forces behind the events that would unfold. As I was already sensing, I would soon know without a doubt that the Palo Santo had its own intelligence and role to play in the story of life, as all things do. My suspicions would also be confirmed: that my personal interest in the tree had somehow enlisted me into its own intentions, and that I had willingly, if unknowingly, become its emissary.

VI

Return to the Equator

As far as I can see, the land is inundated under the unforgiving heavy rains of a changing climate: farms, roads, and homes stand in a watery landscape that portends the dissolution of a habitable world. We are landing in Guayaquil; Sara is at my side.

Six years have passed since my visit to Dante's distillery on the hill above the fishing village. With each passing year, his work as caretaker of the Palo Santo forests of Ecuador has become increasingly important, urgent, and heroic. Dante is famous now in Puerto Lopez and he has received some attention in the Ecuadorian media, but outside of this his exemplary work is barely known to the world.

For the last six years I have dedicated much time to educating people about Dante's mission. I share his fine essential oil distilled from ecologically harvested Palo Santo wood with my audiences, and tell them its story.

The story starts on the beach at Mahabalipuram, where a piece of the sacred wood was offered to the fire and its aroma created the desire to meet the tree. I share how I found myself guided through magical synchronicities to meet the only person in the world who was dedicated to the salvation of this precious species, and the fine artisanal treasure he was producing from it. I go on to tell them how I found the first liter of oil in his little shop on the equator and brought it to the U.S., and how it rapidly became one of our best-selling treasures.

The story continues to the day I received a letter from Dante, informing me that he was ready to start a large-scale reforestation project, requesting financial assistance. I tell my students that I immediately offered to pay twenty-five dollars more for each liter of oil that we purchased from him, and how over the years that money was used to replant hundreds and then thousands of trees.

My audiences then hear of how Dante's work has not only brought the world a great natural medicine from an ancient ethnobotanical source, but has employed many people in a poor village, offering them both financial and social empowerment.

As everyone inhales the uplifting and purifying fragrance of the tree's essence, I point out that this plant-based product represents three types of victory, victories that all of the earth's resources could offer if our culture was enlightened enough to use them wisely: it is a victory for everyone who receives the many therapeutic blessings of this extraordinary oil; it is a victory for the community of people that produce it, who derive an excellent livelihood from sustainably caretaking an endangered species; it is a victory for the tree itself, whose population is now increasing through successful reforestation efforts.

I end the story with a question. Is it possible, I wonder, that a sentient presence, perhaps that of the Palo Santo itself, was behind the remarkable series of coincidences that led to this success story, this story that represents such hope for humanity and nature? Is it possible that a deep and mysterious botanical intelligence made a way for certain predisposed people to come in contact with it, to take up its cause, to assist it, in turn assisting those who cared for it?

Through telling these stories, thousands of people now know about Dante and his work; those people, who have been touched by both his medicine and his vision, have offered great support over the years.

Guayaquil is much the same as last time, except that the taxis and buses are now notorious for robberies; we hire a private driver and start the journey to the north.

A few hours later we arrive at the stunning coastline of Manabi province, the heart of Palo Santo's favorite terrain. Pristine beaches and deep blue water stretch around rocky points; the landscape is desert-like but covered with profuse vegetation. San Pedro cacti are growing on the hillsides, their spiny arms adorned with crimson flowers entwined with the elephantine trunks of the Palo Santo trees.

An hour later we drive into the dusty streets of

Puerto Lopez. The pueblo is mobbed with Ecuadorian tourists, drinking heavily to loud music on the beach.

Dante arrives, bringing his new family to meet us. He was single when I first met him; he had been single a long time, and lonely. Now he strides across the sand hand in hand with his beloved and their sons. A lot of love has come to bless this man, I think, as he greets us and introduces us to Rocio, her son Kevin, and their son Alexandro.

It is the blessings of the Palo Santo, he would tell me many times during this visit.

VII

El Artesan

We arrive at Dante's compound on the hill. It is part distillery, part workshops of his company, El Artesan, part terraced gardens, part shady groves and part family home. The gate is open, as it always is, with a brick pathway inviting us under overhanging branches of a Palo Santo tree. His house is much larger than the last time I saw it: there are more buildings for the artisans, and the nursery extends farther up the hill. Everything is green and flowering, and the air is full of bird songs and the fragrance of the holy tree.

"I remember when I was here last," I say. "It was very dry and there were no trees."

"Yes," Dante replies. "I love all the species of trees, so they grow quickly for me."

There are also more people than the last time, and much more activity. Dante now has a family of his own, not just the adopted children of the neighborhood, and his children have their friends and their collective entourage of pets. Something else is new as well: television and PlayStation.

The Maestro serves us espresso in the communal kitchen. This is where everyone at El Artesan eats, he explains. There is a cook who prepares meals, which everyone shares at a long table. The table, crafted by Dante, is an exquisitely beautiful work of art made from inlaid cross sections of Palo Santo branches of various sizes and colors; the light colored wood is from male trees, we learn, and the dark from females. I would also learn that Dante is not only a master distiller, woodworker and espresso expert but a great chef as well, who sometimes prepares large gourmet meals for his entire staff.

Our tour of El Artesan begins at the far end of the compound, in the wood shed. It is no ordinary woodpile that we find inside, however; this humble structure is a treasure house filled with logs and branches of intensely aromatic Palo Santo wood that is perfuming the entire property with its fresh citrus pine notes.

A middle-aged man of distinctive native Indian appearance is working at a table saw in a side room when we walk in. Dante smiles at my response to the abundance of precious botanical medicine.

"This is the reserve of wood," he says after the roar of the saw has subsided. "At this time of year when there is a lot of rain it is impossible to go into the forest, therefore we keep some wood inside."

He picks up two different branches, explaining again that the light colored type with relatively little aroma is male, while the dark golden yellow type with strong pungency is female.

"These are the branches of Palo Santo," Dante continues. "They have little value in the market because of their size and shape, but look how much oil is concentrated in them." He holds the end of a branch up for closer inspection, and I see that it is richly saturated with aromatic constituents. "This is what we use here to distill the essential oil."

Dante introduces us to Alino, the miller; with the exception of the area protected by his goggles, he is covered from head to foot with perfumed yellow powder. We learn that this gentleman, whose features and aura reveal a calm nobility, has been engaged in the one-pointed concentration of carefully guiding the wood back and forth across the edge of a blade, slowly reducing it to the proper consistency for distillation, for over ten years.

I am curious about this demanding labor, and inquire of Dante why he has settled on this method when other grinding machines could probably work faster and easier. This is not the case, he explains; after trying numerous systems, this method has proven to be the most efficient because the wood has so many variable qualities of hardness and softness, dryness and moisture, and many times it simply turns to a sticky resin. Alino quietly gathers some of the golden treasure for us to examine. We later learn that he works independently and earns three times the typical local wage.

Our next stop is the workshop where the handicrafts and products are made. El Artesan produces several Palo Santo products besides the essential oil, including incense; wood sticks that are used for making tea; soap and shampoo; candles and incense burners. The building is open along the side facing the garden, with a thatched roof and a dirt floor. Boxes of finished products are stacked ready for shipping. Workbenches are covered with projects in various stages of completion and a large collection of unique hand-carved candles. The entire building is suffused with Palo Santo fragrance coming from the products and a small incense burner offering a continuous cloud of mosquito-repelling smoke.

Dante introduces us to a young man sitting at the candle-making bench. I recognize him as the same one who was sitting in the same place making candles six years ago.

"This is Lazaro," he says. "He is like my son. He is very creative, and works in the artistic side of the business."

I quickly learn two more things about Lazaro. The first is that he has been Dante's right hand man for ten years, trained in all the stages of preparing the wood, distillation and manufacturing of products. The second is that he speaks so rapidly and with such a heavy local accent that I need Dante to translate from Spanish to Spanish.

Lazaro's primary job is crafting artisan candles. His creations are extraordinary, reaching three to four feet high, embedded with crystals and carved pieces of Palo Santo wood and cast in multiple colors of wax scented with the sacred oil. These take months to create, he explains, and sell for hundreds of dollars each to clients all over the world.

Sitting with Lazaro is Barbara, Dante's daughter from his first marriage. She has just returned to Puerto Lopez after a long absence, and is delighted to be back at the family business. Like Dante, she does not have good things to say about modern life in her native country, compared to the simple joys of living in a thatched cottage under trees filled with birds, and being able to work with people who truly enjoy their day to day labors.

Our next stop is the distillery. We pause here only briefly to peer inside and to meet Lilliana, who is Dante's chief distiller. We will spend many hours in this room over the coming weeks discussing the details, mysteries and technicalities of the stills and distillation processes, sampling the hydrosols and oils that come at different stages, and doing experiments with new methods.

There are now two tiny rooms, rather than the single room that was here six years ago. Likewise, there are two stills instead of one. The walls are now tiled instead of mud, and there is a small collection of laboratory equipment to complement the glassware of the stills. There is an underground cistern that cools the water passing through the condensers of the stills. Both stills are set closely together in the back room, while the front room is for collecting, pouring and storage of the finished oil and aromatic water.

There is a tantalizing mixture of elements happening inside this little space: the hissing and intense heat from the twin blue flames under the matching shiny stills, the water boiling inside them, the sounds of water cascading into the cool dark cistern under our feet, the rhythm of condensing droplets falling into the separating beakers, the aromas of newly distilled oil mingling with that which has been aging for weeks and months.

In the middle of this stands Lilliana, extremely

pregnant and soon to give birth to her fourth child, calmly decanting another batch of hydrosol from the collecting vessel, patiently pouring it into the large funnel beaker for separation, carefully checking the temperature of the stills. She greets us quietly but her attention is devoted to her work.

"Lilliana has many years of experience with distillation," Dante tells us. "She knows the techniques well, but she also knows things intuitively. She can be in another place doing some other work and can feel if there are problems. She knows the moment to increase the fire, the moment when to reduce the fire."

We stand respectfully in the doorway as she executes the stages of her art and science, and then turn away after a few minutes to follow Dante up the trail. He leads us up the steps to one of the higher terraces, where we stop at a small Palo Santo tree.

"This tree is for David Crow," he says.

"Why?" I ask.

"When I met you six years ago, I felt that it was a very important occasion. You were the first person to help pay for reforestation. I didn't want to continue because there were many problems, but you said 'no problem,' you said 'good, how much is it?' And so I continued with the reforestation projects. For me, you represent the key to a door that is very important for Palo Santo. Therefore I planted these two trees that year, one here and another over there, for this story."

I consider his words, and tell him that by his symbolic action my spirit is connected to his work and this place.

"Yes, of course," he responds. "I am always connected to you and Floracopeia. You were the first one to bring the oil out."

Such are the small life-affirming accomplishments that lighten the heart.

On the uppermost terrace we find a large open workshop, another traditional structure with a thatched roof, woven mat walls and dirt floor. A group of ten women are sitting inside at tables, making cones of Palo Santo incense that will be enjoyed all over the world.

"This group works collectively as an independent business," Dante tells us. "Many of these women have been here at least ten years, like the others we have met. They work as much or as little as they want, and set their own hours."

Our tour of El Artesan is finished. In the

coming days and weeks we will learn more about each aspect of the business, see more that we have not encountered yet, and travel to other communities that are part of Palo Santo's network of livelihood and artistry.

"You have created wonderful abundance here," I say.

"Yes," Dante agrees. "In total there are twenty people, including the ones in the mountains and forest. It requires attention all the time, and I am always watching and asking 'what do you need?' The people are very good quality, and this is most important."

"I have the impression that this is one of biggest businesses in Puerto Lopez," I say.

"No, it is not the biggest," Dante answers, "but it is definitely one of the most novel. It is growing steadily every year.

"I am here all day," the Maestro concludes. "This is my life."

VIII

The Tree of Prosperity

Palo Santo offers two great gifts to humanity:
its important medicinal properties, and its the
economic benefits. Just as the wood and oil alleviate
the suffering of physical and emotional health
problems, the economic benefits derived from this
aromatic tree are medicine for the suffering of
poverty that is endemic to the region where it grows.

In the pueblo of Puerto Lopez a good income
for a family is around $400 a month; many live on
$100 a month. Many families in the countryside
have basic foods from their farms and gardens but
don't have money for clothes or medicines.

The gathering of Palo Santo wood and its sale in local markets has been a source of income for hundreds of years if not longer. Now, distillation of the oil and making handicrafts from the wood are new forms of income and livelihood for local communities, introduced primarily through Dante's pioneering efforts. These products are far more lucrative than selling the wood chips alone, for three reasons. First, they are value-added products; in the case of the oil, the value difference is dramatic. Second, there is a growing local and world market, again as a direct result of Dante's efforts. Third, Dante pays generously and has a progressive and empowering business model.

Dante has found that one large tree can give up to twenty liters of oil, which is worth about $4,000 wholesale to his international clients; it will also give about $2,000 in medicinal sticks, and another $1,000 in incense. This is enough to support seventeen families for one month on normal wages.

Dante currently employs twenty people at El Artesan: five men who live in distant pueblos who collect wood from the forest, the miller of the wood, the two distillers, the ten women who collectively make incense, Lazaro, the primary artist and candle maker, and his daughter Barbara. Collectively, they process and distill between ten and fifteen trees per month and all of them receive much higher than normal local wages, in most cases double to triple.

The progressive and empowering business model of El Artesan is based on Dante's insights into the beneficent qualities of the Palo Santo tree, his interpretation of how the tree would like to be treated and in turn, what gifts it offers. Dante believes that the Palo Santo wants to give many people prosperous right livelihood and that when people come in contact with the essence of the tree, whether it is in the form of its essential oil or its fragrant wood, it has a deeply transformative effect, including nurturing, activating and manifesting their creative and spiritual potential. Therefore, his approach to growing his enterprise has not followed the typical exploitative model of a hierarchical business.

"Nobody here works by the day," Dante explained. "Everybody works according to the quantity they produce. This is a project to empower people, to lead them to self-sufficiency, independence, and autonomy. I am not a nail to hold them, because they are free people, professionals."

Dante begins this empowerment by offering people training, which he has done freely and generously in several communities; he then places those trained people in positions as independent artisans who produce finished products that he purchases and assists them to grow and maintain their own businesses. El Artesan, therefore, is a collective of entrepreneurs and artisans who have complete autonomy, who sell their finished products to Dante, whether it is the wood collectors, the wood miller, the distillers, the incense makers, or those who make candles and other products.

One of the most important results of this system is that the members of El Artesan are able to work at jobs that are safe, healthy and well paid. Raising the income level is especially significant for the women, who are a majority of those working there. Being well paid gives them increased authority in the family – a development that challenges traditional norms. In many South American communities men do not want women to have independent employment outside the labors of the home: if they work they will have money, and if they have money they will have more freedom.

Preventing women from developing their own careers is one of the ways that patriarchal societies have kept women disempowered, but this disempowerment is also the root of poverty within those societies.

Another result of Dante's progressive business model is that he is highly respected and appreciated in his community. Everyone in town knows him, and everyone knows he is wealthy by local standards. Whenever Sara and I would take a taxi home from the beach, we would just say "Dante Bolcato," and every driver knew where he lived. Being known by all and also being a foreigner who is financially well off, however, is not without its potential dangers in a third world country.

The hillside where El Artesan and Dante's residence are located is a neighborhood with nice homes owned by relatively affluent international residents, including Italians, Canadians, and Germans. The surrounding neighborhood is very poor. When we first walked into Dante's home, the first thing he did was demonstrate that the doors and windows had no locks and that couches were everywhere.

"Look," he said. "This is my house, but it is

open for everyone. Renato's house, robbers came. Giuseppe's house, robbers came. Michel's house, robbers came; he had to construct a three-meter high fence all around to protect it.

"My house, no problem, everything is open for everyone. It is very protected here, because the people protect me, my children, my family. This is because of Palo Santo. It has been like this for many years, so it is true."

IX

Home on the Hill

Sara and I settle into our new home on the hill. The house, while being quite high end by local standards, is not worth describing, other than we are grateful to have cold showers in the heat of the afternoon; the other notable plumbing feature is that when it rains, which it does almost every night, it also rains inside.

Our new residence, as one would predict in the tropics, is also home to a number of creatures, including cockroaches the size of small mangoes and intriguing looking spiders. There is an abundance of mosquitoes, and for the few days before we locate a net to hang lopsidedly from various wall fixtures, we sit directly in the breeze of a small fan or in thick clouds of Palo Santo smoke, and resign ourselves to waking with evidence of a feast having taken place on and of our flesh. Dante warns us that the cumulative toxicity of the ferocious insects is definitely not healthy, as we find ourselves increasingly irritable and agitated. The neighbor informs us about another unique danger, niguas, parasitic fleas that burrow under toenails to lay their eggs; her story is particularly graphic, as she recently had to have a nigua surgically removed after her entire leg became infected.

But these are all a normal part of life, and other than almost stepping on a scorpion with bare feet in the dark, fade quickly into irrelevance. What is more notable is what takes place outside the house, in the spectacular vista that unfolds below and away from our little open deck facing the village, the bay with its fishing boats coming and going, the mountain point where waves crash against cliffs, and the ocean's ever-changing horizon.

Mornings bring either brilliant blazing sunlight foretelling an intensely hot day or a temporary reprieve of gentle gray cloudscapes accompanied by mists, rain and pleasant breezes. The midday sun is almost always punishing, producing the paradoxical effect of causing humans to become lethargic and flies to become hyperactive. Afternoons bring more cooling breezes and the daily spectacle of slowly developing majestic equatorial sunsets, always at the same time: purples and violets reflecting on towering cloud pillars, rays of golden yellows streaming across the bay, pinks and reds reflected on the dark waves.

Throughout the day and night there is a cacophony of sound that drifts up to our perch. First come the calls and songs of birds, delightfully refreshing in their unfamiliarity. As morning unfolds, vendors make their rounds in pickup trucks armed with loudspeakers announcing various items for sale, including bottled water and fresh cheeses. In the afternoon the sounds of village life predominate, with children playing in the dirt streets, three-wheel taxis honking at each other and the locals coming and going on their motorcycles.

Evenings bring the real excitement. A quiet night is a tapestry of animal languages, drones and chirps of insects, frogs that sound like cats, cats fighting, dogs spreading the word about the latest events; sometimes, in a rare moment we can hear the tide turning down on the beach, or a faraway thunder storm.

Most nights are not tranquil, however, because the residents of Puerto Lopez love music, fiestas, and alcohol. From our window we can often hear at least four or five simultaneous parties, each with a live band and a drunken emcee, all within a few blocks and persisting until dawn. As could be imagined, gaiety is only half the story of life, and there are also the sounds of enraged arguments, sirens and an occasional car crash, which sometimes knocks out a power line and thus ends another over-amplified revelry.

There is not much to do in this town of a few dusty streets, but we did not come here for that. For the first week we mostly avoid the beach because it is "Carnival," which is nothing like the vivid artistic bacchanalia of Brazil except for the thievery. After that we make evening forays to the malecon, the road along the beachfront, to check out what dining opportunities are available, having wearied of the extremely limited selection of produce from the local open market and pastas from the miniature version of the SuperMaxi. We find that we have our choice of a few Italian flavored versions of the same limited produce and pastas, a few delectable ceviche dishes fresh off the boats, and a variety of promising-looking places that are never open.We settle into a simple routine of oatmeal and lilikois for breakfast, take advantage of the lunches served at Dante's house, and resign ourselves to gratitude for another pizza on the malecon.

To me, Dante's work is immensely interesting, a stellar example of a project that deserves the world's attention. Set against the gritty backdrop of Puerto Lopez, it is not surprising that there would be nothing to do on a daily basis except spend time with the Maestro.

And so we become the guests who return over and over, walking the short distance between our homes every morning and back every evening. Dante is always pleased with our arrival, always accommodating, always generous with his time in the midst of ongoing work and visitors, and always has a new plan for another trip to the forest or another distillation experiment. I usually have new questions after a night of transcribing the lectures of the previous day, but even if I don't, the conversation immediately becomes animated and engaging. His mind is full of new ideas, mine is full of inspiration and enjoyment of learning, and we have an easy chemistry of intellectual camaraderie. I often sense that he is as pleased by my questions and attention and interest in his work as I am by his teachings and accomplishments.

X

Here I Stay

One of the great mysteries that lingered in my mind after meeting Dante the first time was his past, and the conditions that brought him to Puerto Lopez. I was intrigued by the brief biography that he had given me, which had left me with the impression that he possessed unique healing powers.

He had been a psychotherapist, I recalled, and had been able to help and cure many people. I remembered that he had mentioned that he had some type of ability to cure people of addictions, so I had assumed that he was either skilled as a hypnotherapist, had some kind of charismatic power of suggestion or psychic influence, or both. I also knew that in spite of his abilities to help others, the primary reason he came to Ecuador was because he was unhappy with his life in Italy, and sick from stress, exhaustion and his own addictions. During our first meeting, he had said that he had been a heavy smoker.

Inquiring about his personal story was foremost in my mind when Sara and I arrived at Dante's house on the first day. After our tour of the distillery and workshops, he ushered us into the top floor of his house, where he lives with Rocio and their sons. The house is a six-sided structure built around a huge tree trunk set in the middle of the main room. The ceiling is a geometric pattern of converging beams, the walls and floor are of luxuriant wood, and the huge windows facing all directions are perpetually open. A wide balcony circles the entire perimeter, giving stunning views of the village and bay through the cooling trees.

We settle into chairs on the balcony, and the Maestro appreciates my description of his architecture as the "home of a visionary."

"Are you content?" I ask.

"Yes, very content," he replies. "This is a time

of my life that is very, very good."

From what I have seen so far, he has ample reason to be happy and he appears that way. But it was not always like that, I mention, remembering our conversation from six years ago.

He agrees. "I came here because I was tired of Italy. I was depressed and alone, and it was a dark time. I was single, and my children had grown. I was tired of my work as a psychotherapist, it was not stimulating."

Dante shifts to storyteller, as he will often do, and acts out his tiresome work routine.

"Hello doctor.

"What do you want?

"I want to stop smoking.

"Ok, now you are cured."

"Do you have some special healing power or ability with hypnotherapy?" I ask, after wondering for many years.

He avoids the question, simply saying that he worked in family practice.

"But you had a lot of success," I press on.

"Yes, but it was not good for me."

How my new teacher actually cured people would be left to my imagination, but in the coming weeks my observations would confirm that he was a man who positively influenced everyone with his cheerful, generous, gregarious and enthusiastic presence and demeanor.

Dante worked for many years in a government-sponsored clinic, he explains. He describes how he came to Ecuador seeking a new life, and the various places where he went in search of a home: Quito, Cuenca, and others, but nothing appealed to him. Then he came to Puerto Lopez, in January of 2000. Events transpired to keep him here; perhaps it was the work of the Palo Santo.

"A few days after I arrived here there was a presidential assassination and coup of the government. They closed all the roads and the airport. I could not leave."

Dante motions to the sky above our balcony perch. The turkey vultures are circling over the village, as they do all day everyday, while down along the beach the frigatebirds are gliding back and forth.

"I was stuck here in Puerto Lopez. The first day, I look at the birds. They are soaring over the beach. I start thinking, and looking around, and noticing things. The wind current is coming from the ocean. There is a mountain here on this side of the bay, another there on that side, and those three in the back. The wind and air are very pure and good. The current of the atmosphere cleans everything. I said 'This is very good for me.'

"The second day I was walking on the beach. The fishermen were bringing in a lot of fish. The children all had fish, everyone had enough to eat. I said 'this is what I want, freedom from poverty.'

"The third day I did an experiment. I sat down in the center of town, closed my eyes, listened and took notes about what people were saying. I listened to all the words, I wrote them all down. The words that were used the most were 'more or less,' and 'ya mismo.' I looked in the dictionary. 'Ya mismo' is a phrase that refers to a time that does not exist."

Dante stands up and begins pacing back and forth, looking at imaginary watches.

"When I was a psychologist in Italy I had to wear two watches, one for actual time and one for the paid time of my patients. My life was crazy, running here and there, controlled by time. I lived in a building for twenty years where no one knew their neighbors. I lived like this for almost forty years.

"But then I started listening to the people here.

If you ask 'When does the bus arrive?' they won't say at eight or nine, they will say 'Ya mismo.' Everything is 'more or less.'

"Then I noticed that the people of Puerto Lopez don't wear watches. That is what convinced me. I started thinking, 'these people live in a time and space that does not exist.' I said to myself 'this place is good to live. No more crazy.'"

But it was the tree that ultimately had the greatest influence.

"On the fourth day I went to visit the Palo Santo forest. My guide gave me a little branch of it to smell."

Dante holds an imaginary stick of the sacred wood to his nose, inhaling deeply.

"This was my dream," he says, inhaling again, enraptured.

"I want to live here for this, for Palo Santo."

Two months later, he was able to leave the country and return to Italy. He put his affairs in order there, then came back to his new home. Now, twelve years have passed.

"Here I am," he concludes. "Here I stay, with Palo Santo."

XI

Palo Santo

What was this tree that had the power to captivate Dante's mind and heart to the extent that he would dedicate his life to it? What was this arboreal species that had enough significance in my own life to make a journey of thousands of miles to learn about its secrets?

Palo Santo, the "holy stick," is the name that was given to the species Bursera graveolens by the Spanish; originally, they first called it Palo Dulce, "sweet stick." The genus Bursera is named after the botanist Joachim Burser, who lived from 1583 to 1649; graveolens is Latin for "heavy, penetrating odor." I was familiar with both of these terms from studies of other aromatic plants, such as Pelargonium graveolens (geranium) and Bursera microphyla ("small leafed"), the elephant tree of the Southwest desert that gives the incense resin generically called copal.

Palo Santo grows throughout Central and South America, from Mexico in the north to Peru, Brazil and Paraguay in the south. The terrain where I met the tree is the tropical dry forest of coastal Ecuador, in the Machalilla Park where Dante first encountered it. This region is considered to be the heart of Palo Santo's territory, which contains what is probably the largest remaining population of the trees in the world. This ecosystem is generally dry and hot nine months out of the year, with a subtle cooling fog that comes from the ocean; from January through March there is a short monsoon season with periodic torrential rains and increased heat.

Because of its environment the tree is adapted to go for long periods without water, and can then grow quickly when the rains come; in this way it is similar to desert trees. The natives say that the tree can live for fifty years without water. This is not surprising since Palo Santo belongs to the same family as frankincense and myrrh, and one can see similarities between their appearances, especially the growth of the trunk.

The tree does not have a long tap root, but instead has long superficial roots that allow it to absorb water quickly; this is also similar to frankincense of the dry deserts, which is some cases have no roots at all, just a base that attaches to rocks. Palo Santo trees have long branches and short trunks, which make them very top heavy. The trees are prone to falling over, especially during seasons when there is heavy rain.

The tree flowers, fruits and produces seeds all within a few weeks after the onset of the rainy season. Small flowers appear for a very short period of time in January and February, and the seeds come in March and April. Seeds and fruits are a major source of food for birds.

According to Dante, the number of leaves on

the tree is variable: when there are abundant rains, the tree produces leaves in clusters of nine, when there is less they come in clusters of six, and during dry periods three.

One of the first stories that Dante told me when I met him six years ago was about how there are both male and female trees. He explained that the trees live in groups of eight or nine females with one male. The males can live up to three hundred years, while the females generally live eighty to ninety years. I found this curious and did some research, but was unable to find anything that confirmed this. I suspected Dante's mystical imagination might be at work, but at the same time it was one of the subjects I wanted to discuss further.

I asked him to describe the male and female trees again on the first day after returning to Puerto Lopez; he stated again that this was true. He went on to explain that this information was known to the indigenous people and that he had confirmed it, but that botanists either did not know or did not agree. He said that according to botanists, both types of trees have the same leaves, the same flowers, the same fruits and seeds, and are therefore not different species.

There are, however, other characteristics that qualify them as male and female, and might possibly represent two different varieties of the Bursera graveolens species.

The trees that are considered male, besides living longer, produce a much smaller quantity of flowers, fruits and seeds, and therefore have few seedlings growing underneath them. The females, on the other hand, produce an abundance of flowers, fruits and seeds and have large populations of seedlings growing under them. Additionally, because the males live longer, they grow to be much larger than the females.

Unlike other aromatic trees such as sandalwood or cedar which have a content of essential oil that gradually increases in their trunk and heartwood as they get older, or trees such as eucalyptus which have oil-rich leaves, a Palo Santo tree does not have essential oil in a usable form in either the wood or leaves. The green branches and leaves have a light aroma of the oil, but these are not distilled. If the trunk is scarred it will bleed a resin, which is collected after it has congealed and used in medicine, but the tree does not produce a resin that is harvested and used like frankincense or copal.

Curiously, a living tree is not a source of either the aromatic wood or the essential oil that is distilled from it.

If there is no aromatic oil inside a living tree, then where does it come from? This was one of the greatest mysteries of Palo Santo, giving its life cycle mythological and symbolic dimensions.

The formation of the oil inside the heartwood begins after the tree dies and falls to the ground, and becomes increasingly concentrated as the years pass. However, not all dead trees produce oil: if a tree is cut, it will not produce oil, nor will it produce oil if it dies from disease. A Palo Santo tree will produce oil only if it dies a natural death.

After a natural death a tree will stay standing for several years. Eventually it will fall from the passage of time or from wind or heavy rain. The process of producing oil will begin after the tree has been on the ground for some time. The oil will develop gradually inside the trunk. The longer the tree remains on the ground, the better the quality and the higher the quantity of oil that it will contain. A tree must lie on the ground at least three years, and preferably six, before it can be distilled.

As one might imagine, this process is highly symbolic. The symbolism of rebirth after death is one of the primary archetypal motifs connected to Palo Santo that Dante stressed again and again: the wood and its oil are great medicines that give life, and they express the tree's life force that has undergone resurrection after its death.

To make the story even more intriguing, it is the females that produce the most oil, while the male trees produce very little, even with their greater longevity. The wood of male trees is a light white color, indicating little oil content, while the female wood is yellow to golden brown, indicating saturation with the oil.

In describing the female trees and their fullness of oil, Dante would frequently refer to them as pregnant. Their feminine nature can also be seen in their production of abundant seeds and the large number of seedlings growing under their outstretched limbs.

The Palo Santo tree unites two powerful archetypes: the life-giving nourishing Mother, and death/rebirth. It symbolically expresses both the story of Jesus's death and resurrection, a dominant religious image in the collective Catholic consciousness of South America, and the older matriarchal goddess images of earlier cultures. It is for this reason, my teacher would emphatically repeat, that the tree has the name "Santo."

XII

The Jealous Tree

I had known for some time that a mysterious force lay at the root of so many synchronistic events surrounding my relationship with Palo Santo. My interpretation of these events was that the tree had introduced itself to me on a beach in India, had made arrangements for me to meet it in Ecuador, then to meet its oil at Dante's, then to assist in bringing that precious essence to the market in the U.S., and now to make this return journey. I had not had much insight into the nature of its intelligence, other than what I had observed happening over the years: the development of a network of people linked by a series of intriguing coincidences, resulting in a growing movement to support reforestation of the tree. The tree, I told people repeatedly, was looking for people to help it replant itself.

Although I knew on some level that Palo Santo, like all plants, had some kind of botanical personality, I never considered what it might be, other than powerful. It was intriguing to learn from Dante that this species has a distinct reputation among the people that have lived with it and utilized it for centuries: it was jealous and protective.

"Palo Santo is very interesting," Dante says. We are gathered around the long table in the communal kitchen, sharing a meal with the members of El Artesan.

"The native people say that the tree loves you a lot. They say that if you put it on the body for pain, you are putting on protection. It wants to hold you. If you put it on your neck and shoulders, it is like pulling your jacket around your neck. If you drink the tea for flu, you should not go outside, you should not go dancing, you should go to bed and sleep. But Palo Santo is also very possessive."

As is often the case, my limited but rapidly expanding Spanish vocabulary necessitates discussion to clarify what exactly Dante means. In this case, everyone gets involved in a lively discussion about the meaning of the word "celoso." Lazaro, as always, has the most graphic and comic illustrations.

"Celoso is when you don't want other people to look at your woman," Dante explains. "This possessiveness is very important, because the tree wants you to respect it. It wants you to do things for it.

"I love the tree a lot. Because I teach about reforestation and how it should be shared with everyone, Palo Santo wants me a lot."

I find this intriguing, but it makes perfect sense. If you love a person, he or she becomes protective of your love, and the same happens with animals, so why would it not be that way with plants? I was curious how a plant could express this kind of sentiment.

"Palo Santo does not want me to produce any other kind of oil," Dante responds. "I tried to distill guava leaves, which have an oil that is very good for digestive problems; I had problems with the still, and had to spend money to get it fixed. I tried to produce lemongrass, but many bad things started to happen in my life and work."

"The Palo Santo is controlling your life," I comment.

"Yes, the Palo Santo is controlling my life," Dante agrees.

I am reminded of stories of spiritual people who dedicated their lives to worshipping a particular deity, who in turn bestowed various blessings on them, but also obstacles and consequences for neglecting their vows and devotions.

"To work with the Palo Santo you have to have a great vision," the Maestro concludes. "Its roots are in the earth and the branches are in the universe. You have to be very careful, and you have to pay a lot of attention.

"Therefore, I am also protective. When you go to the forest and you get the wood in your arms, it is like holding a baby. You put it over here, where nobody can see it, and you feel possessive. When you are distilling the oil and then put it in the bottle, you want to put the lid on immediately, because you feel protective.

"This is not a passionate love; it is a love with

respect. I take no more than I need. I don't throw away or waste anything; I use the roots, the trunk, and the branches, even the little ones."

XIII

The Forest

We arrive at Los Frailes beach in the
Machalilla Park. As soon as we step out of the truck
we are surrounded by swarms of relentless
mosquitoes, but Dante does not seem to notice. He
begins telling me about each of the individual trees
that are in the parking area, as if they were old

friends.

"This is a tree that I was investigating twelve years ago," he says, pointing to the one closest to where we have parked. "You can see that the roots are superficial, the trunk is short, and the branches are very long."

Dante goes to another tree and points with his walking stick to the same features. "You can see that the branches are very big and heavy. This is what causes them to fall down in the rain."

Within minutes we are drenched with sweat from the humid heat, and I understand why he is carrying a towel.

Doves are calling from the treetops. The Maestro is obviously happy to be back in the forest, which although close to his home, he does not often visit. He seems to know everyone here and is already waving and exchanging greetings and smiles with people strolling by. He is also enjoying being on camera, a local celebrity.

"How old is this one?" I ask.

"This is about sixty or seventy years."

It seems to me that for the size of the tree, they must grow rapidly.

"It depends on the amount of rain that falls in

one year," Dante explains. "This is very specific to the dry forest. In this rainy period of the year, January through April, the tree is waking up, it produces leaves, it is green. Later, June through December, the climate is foggy, like a very subtle rain. My belief is that the root system allows the tree to grow after the rains; at that time of year the tree grows in height and width."

Dante pulls down a low hanging branch and runs his fingers through the lush foliage as he talks.

"This tree is a female. Every previous year it has made a lot of seeds, but this year, with a lot of rain, there are no seeds. But the tree is growing a lot; therefore, this year the tree is thinking 'it is better for me to grow,' and it is not thinking about producing children."

Dante walks to another tree.

"You can see that this is a year of abundance: it has leaves in sevens; when there is not much rain the leaves are in fives, and when there is no rain they are in threes.

"Palo Santo has a memory. It can live a long time without water. It has the capacity to relax, to go dormant for a long time. The natives say this tree can live more than fifty years without water. This is normal for plants of the desert, and also for plants of the dry forest."

We start walking, trying to escape the mosquitoes that are devouring us. At the entrance to the beach more friends greet Dante with salutations and exchanges of news and stories. Gorgeous but seductively treacherous waves are breaking on the white sand, where a few tourists are sunbathing in the scorching equatorial heat. We make our way toward a steep hill covered with Palo Santo trees.

We reach the trail and start climbing into the foliage and up the mountain. Soon I am breathing heavily, but the Maestro keeps up a fast pace, pounding his walking stick on the ground to warn the snakes of our arrival. Dante shows us unique species along the way: plants with leaves that look like coins, trees with branches that bend like rubber without breaking.

We come to a massive Palo Santo tree.

"Wait here," Dante instructs. He walks forward toward the tree, turns to face us and announces dramatically, "I want to present the Mother of Palo Santo."

She is indeed a majestic tree. Three major trunks arch over us, providing welcome shade. A gigantic mud termite nest is built along one of the larger branches directly above the trail.

"This is over a hundred years old," he says, "probably one hundred and thirty. It is unique; it is a female, but it is very, very rare to find one this old. We will meet some other old ones in this area, but they are very difficult to find in other parts of the forest."

Dante examines the trunk carefully.

"This is a tree I call 'The Mother.' Here we can see a history of the past. When a father was expecting a child, two weeks before it arrived he would come here with a machete."

Dante demonstrates hacking one of the trunks with his stick. I come to inspect closely and see that it is covered with hundreds of scars.

"For medicine. The tree gives a resin, and they put that on the umbilicus of the newborn. This is a ritual for benediction, from the past culture. The fathers now don't do this; they go to the pharmacy."

We rest for a few minutes, leaning on the massive trunks and enjoying the shade. I think of days long past, when native people would make the pilgrimage through the forest to this tree to gather its resin, use it ritualistically, and benefit from its undoubtedly antimicrobial benefits.

Dante strides to the perimeter of the shade and points with his walking stick.

"Here we can see the roots. When the tree dies, these roots are very, very strong with oil, and the oil is very, very strong. It is not like oil, but concentrated like resin. It is concentrated a lot in the roots and the branches."

We proceed along the trail. Dante suddenly stops and begins hitting the shrubbery with his stick, making loud noises. He hacks his way into the underbrush and disappears. I follow, and find him bent over a trunk that is covered with vines.

"This is a tree that died twelve years ago," he announces.

He stretches his arms out.

"It was this big across, another Mother. But now, there is nothing left. It did not make any oil."

Dante pokes at the rotten trunk.

"Why not? I ask.

"Because not all trees give oil," he says emphatically, waving his finger at me for forgetting what he has said before. He repeats his earlier teachings.

"Out of every six trees, three are good for oil,

and three are not. When the tree dies of a sickness it does not give oil. When it dies from a machete it does not give oil. It gives this."

He pounds on the decomposing trunk with his stick, showing how it turns to brown powder.

"I killed this one," he says.

"You?"

"Yes, me. I did it, in January of 2000, for investigation. No oil. It is not possible to cut a tree and get oil. It doesn't work. This is the result. The oil only comes when the tree dies a natural death and does not have a disease."

We scramble back to the trail and stand in the blistering sun. Dante is unfazed.

"There is a relationship between life and death," he says solemnly. "The tree that dies without disease later gives an oil that benefits life. In this way Palo Santo lives on, and life is love, and love is life. There is also a relationship between the power that Palo Santo has to clean bad energy, and the power to benefit life."

The Maestro bows after his short oration.

"Please," he says, motioning us to follow him further up the steep incline. He stops a moment later and turns.

"The fantastic part, the marvelous and wondrous part, is that this tree dies to give its life. What other tree in world does this?"

We continue. The trail is surrounded by increasingly lush floral growth. Dante points out more uses of the various plants; here is one that is now being cultivated for biodiesel used on the Galapagos.

We come to an open stretch that looks over the forest. A choir of tropical birds is singing in the foliage.

"Here we have a number of Palo Santo trees," Dante says, "fifty to sixty trees per hectare." He points to the profusion of trunks, entwined with San Pedro cactus.

We stand for some time, listening to the bird songs and sound of the waves from below, catching our breath.Soon we are climbing again through areas exposed to the stunning heat. We come to a cliff and catch our first view of the coast to the north.

"Here we have a lot of trees," Dante says, waving his stick over the valley below. He points to a small grove at the edge of the trail. "Here is one that is seventy or eighty years old. Here is one that is twenty years old. Here is one that is ten years old.

Here is one that is five."

"A family," I comment.

"Yes, but this is very important to understand, because it is a vision of how much wood we have. This year we will have this old one, then later we will have that younger one. This is important for the reforestation plan."

"It is the future of the tree," I say.

"It is. It is a vision that allows me to think that tomorrow we are going to have Palo Santo."

We push on. Overhead, the trees weave a dense canopy of winding branches. Dante picks a fruit from a San Pedro cactus and savors it.

"There are many dead trees here," he says. A minute later he calls from the undergrowth. I follow him and discover a huge trunk, hard and yellow in the sun. He beats it with his stick to show that it is solid, with no rot.

"This one is good for oil," he comments. "It has been dead eight years, and was more or less a hundred twenty years old when it died. It has fragrance, the branches, everything. With a tree like this, we can produce twenty liters of oil. It is very good."

The trail stretches ahead. The Maestro does

not seem affected by the heat or the steep climb.

"Where exactly is the equator?" I ask the next time we pause.

"The line is right here," he says, tracing it with his stick.

"Does this mean anything to you?" I wonder.

"The significance is that the sun comes up at six in the morning and goes down at six in the evening, every day of the year. Therefore we have twelve hours of light and twelve hours of night. This is a very good therapy for human beings; I believe that it helps those of us who live here to find equilibrium. The temperature is very good, because all year you only need this light shirt; there is no cold, no heat."

"No heat?" I ask, wiping more sweat from my face. Sara is waiting in a spot of shade, looking flushed.

"No heat, no cold," Dante responds. "This is a very good therapy. I think it is like a hospital for cleaning and healing the body."

"That is why you are youthful."

"More every day," he agrees.

"That is why you have more energy than me. You can walk up the hill very fast and I can barely follow."

"I am sixty years old now," Dante says "When I first came here I was forty-eight and I was very tired. When I first came here, walking on this trail, I was like this..."

He bends over his walking stick and pants heavily, like I have been.

"But now, no. This is from living at the center of the earth. This is very good medicine for me."

We finally arrive at the observatory tower at the top of the hill. It is shaded by a thatch roof and open to the breezes coming from the intensely blue ocean. The vista in all directions is spectacular, stretching far to the north and south along the coast, and across a vast expanse of Palo Santo forest to the east.

Dante has spent a lot of time alone at this lookout, he tells us. The whales come here, just below, to make love.

"Look over here," he calls.

He gestures over the green landscape to the east.

"This is the forest where we collect the wood for producing the Palo Santo oil for Floracopeia. It comes from here. This is where your trees are, the trees that you paid for reforestation."

There is a unique feeling that fills the heart from seeing the results of many people working together to restore nature's beauty, from helping a forest become abundant and healthy, and from knowing that from this abundance comes a beautiful perfume of healing, offered by a tree in its death.

XIV

Reforestation

There is a sign outside of Dante's small shop on the beach front road, with two statements summing up his philosophy of life: "I believe that planting a tree saves my life," and "Always think good things are going to happen."

In Dante's mind, the blessings of love, health and abundance that have come into his life, like a rebirth as he approached his sixth decade, are gifts from Palo Santo; these gifts have come, he believes, as a direct result of his vision, mission and intention to care for the tree. The tree, he says, loves and protects those who love and protect it; this love and protection takes many forms, from keeping away mosquitoes, to preventing and treating illness, to being a source of economic prosperity.

But that love and protection goes much further, Dante feels, to the very core of whether a distiller will even be able to work with the tree at all, or whether its sentient intelligence will cause obstacles that will cause the distiller to abandon the effort. There are many cases, he told me, of people who have attempted to make their fortunes from the distillation of Palo Santo oil who have failed, simply because they do not have the underlying motivation to care for the tree, and in turn, the tree has no love or protection for them. Those failures are due to many things, ranging from lack of practical knowledge to strange misfortunes, such as stills exploding, befalling those whose aim is purely self-enrichment.

Dante believes that the success of El Artesan is due entirely to the reciprocal relationship that exists between his efforts to replant the Palo Santo forests and the tree's subsequent approval, support and blessings. This belief is like the mythological thinking that underlies many rituals and ceremonies to invoke the blessings of deities, but it is supported empirically by two undeniable facts: the continued success of his endeavors, and the remarkable synchronicity that surrounds his work and events in his personal life.

Besides his love for the tree and his faith in its reciprocal protection, there is a practical reason Dante is motivated to replant the Palo Santo: the long-term availability of trees for distillation. Currently, his distillery requires between ten to fifteen dead trees per month. He has a ten-year contract with the Ecuadorian government to harvest this wood from various tracts of land, including the Machalilla Park, and he estimates that he has many years of future supplies remaining.

But Palo Santo is not a tree that can be grown in plantations and harvested for its oil as it matures, like tea tree, which is cultivated as a row crop; an entire intact forest is necessary to produce trees that live their full life span, die naturally and free of diseases, and then age for many years on the forest floor. Therefore, replanting of Palo Santo is an effort that will span generations, and it will be Dante's grandsons who will distill the trees that he plants in his lifetime.

In Dante's mind, the availability of the wood

for distillation is a secondary concern; it is the renewal of entire forests for their own sake that is the primary goal. Like most species of trees, Palo Santo has been heavily exploited, and the population of trees has declined dramatically because of heavy logging. When I asked Dante about the extent of the damage, he replied: "Deserts. Many regions that were once forest are now desert." If the forests are to survive, a large-scale sustained reforestation effort is needed.

The primary reason the trees have been cut is because they are excellent firewood. Although a living tree does not have essential oil that can be distilled, it contains resins that make the wood burn very hot; this has made it a desirable wood for industrial purposes. Specifically, it has fueled the brick making and fish oil industries in Ecuador, both of which consumed massive amounts. Now, brick making has been replaced by cement, and the fish oil industry has changed from using wood fire to diesel for cooking. In spite of these improvements, the tree is still being cut heavily for firewood.

The process of reforestation starts in Dante's nursery. I witnessed the beginning of this work the first time I visited his home on the hillside. At that time, there were a few bare terraces under simple shade structures and a few potted saplings. Every few months I would receive photos of the progress: a few more potted trees, a new terrace, more trees, another terrace. Now, there are five thousand saplings in pots under awnings on terraces climbing up the hill behind his house, waiting for new homes.

While being relatively small, this is probably the largest nursery of Palo Santo trees in the world; I learned from Eric, who is well acquainted with environmental causes, that Dante is probably the only person in the country, if not South America, dedicated to such an effort. For this, he has been featured on national television, and his distillery is now receiving an increased amount of visitors and clients from around the world.

About a year ago I received a remarkable message from the Maestro.

"I am very emotional," he said. "After six years of trying, I germinated the seed of the Palo Santo. It is a great Christmas gift, and you can see a picture on Facebook."

Most likely, this was a first in the world of botany, as the seed of Palo Santo requires complex conditions to germinate.

The journey of the little saplings from the terraces of Dante's nursery back to the forest is complicated. It is an important part of the story that I have been sharing with audiences, because Floracopeia has been collaborating with El Artesan by contributing funds from the sale of the oil for reforestation. However, there were many developments that occurred over the years, and the language barrier in our communications prevented me from clearly understanding the complexities of the project. This is not surprising, considering that it involves working with local communities, with the government, with NGO's, and with fundraising.

The short version of the story is that Dante has succeeded in replanting about forty times as many trees as he has taken out of the forest over the last seven years. How that was done, and how it will continue to be done, is not a simple story.

When I first met Dante six years ago, he was already starting work on germination of trees, but had not started any reforestation yet. I strongly encouraged him, by offering to pay extra money for each liter of oil for that purpose. With those initial funds he planted six hundred trees in the Los Frailes area of the park; this was the landscape that he pointed out to us from the mountaintop during our trek through the forest.

After this phase he worked with an NGO that assisted him with the planting of 40,000 trees in various areas around the region. At that time, our funds were incorporated into that larger project. This project was recently completed.

Now, the reforestation project is about to go into a new phase, improved by lessons learned from the previous efforts.

Dante has given proposals to the Ecuadorian government, and he has had meetings with representatives from the Ministry of the Environment about them. If his proposals are enacted, the government will designate unused areas of land as forest preserves, and employ a forest warden at each of these areas. In exchange, the government will use the project for its publicity campaigns about its role in preserving the environment; this is highly appealing to the current administration, as it is working to publicize Ecuador as a country with a strong agenda of ecological preservation.

Currently, there is a team of wood harvesters who bring the Palo Santo to El Artisan for distillation. Under the new plan, they would also be paid to take saplings from the nursery and plant them in the regions they are harvesting; this would not only increase the population of the trees, but enhance the income of the harvesters as well.

Dante's goal is two-fold; the first is to replant the trees. However, he considers the second goal even more important: to generate an attitude of pride and responsibility in those who are caretaking the trees. He explains this simply: "The people who are planting the trees will become the official paid caretakers of the forest, which will be the true protection."

On his side, Dante will have a license to collect the wood for distillation. All his products will contain notices that a certain percentage of the income goes to the reforestation effort, thereby generating further funding.

No matter what the outcome of this phase of reforestation, or even the long-term outcome of this particular species of tree, there is profound wisdom to consider in Dante's simple philosophy that guides his relationship with nature, written on a sign on a dusty street in an equatorial fishing village: "I believe that planting a tree saves my life." In my mind, it is a prophetic message for humanity.

XV

Bees and Bats

Our topic of discussion--the various creatures that live in the Palo Santo forest--starts because of an exotic drink that Dante serves us, to quench the thirst of another intensely hot and humid day.

"There is a unique species of bee that lives in the dry forest," our teacher begins. "It lives in hives that are four feet underground. These bees are tiny, and do not sting. They are very difficult to find, because they only come out at night."

I reflect on the different species of bees I have met in various parts of the world. I remember clay hives hung in trees in the jungles of South India that are home to a tiny stingless bee that works during the day, and a subterranean species of wasp that produces a powerful medicinal honey in the same part of the world, but I cannot recall one like this.

"There is a special skill that is needed to find them," Dante continues, "because you have to listen very carefully for the sound of a single bee in the dark. The ability to find these bees is partly based on hearing them, but it is more based on feeling them through the heart."

Dante puts his hand to his heart and stands in silence for a moment. The sound of the wood grinder comes from the shed, conversations of the women drift down from the upper terrace, the tropical birds call. Palo Santo smoke drifts upward from its home in the large earthen bowl in the center of the room. A thunderstorm is approaching.

The Maestro calls to Lazaro to bring refreshment.

"Sixto has the ability to find the bees," he continues. I had met Sixto briefly during my first visit; he is one of the men who gather wood from the forest for distillation.

"Sixto has ten brothers; their father taught all of them how to find the bees, but only he can do it."

To gather the honey of this rare and elusive bee, one must dig a large hole around the hive, which can take a full day. Once the hive is exposed, it is like gathering other kinds of honey in the wild, except that the bees are docile; they leave the hive, dig a new burrow, and make a new hive.

"What flowers do these bees harvest?" I wonder.

"They gather the nectar of the San Pedro cactus, from both the flowers and the fruits," Dante replies. "The cactus blooms at night, so that is why the bees come out then."

Lazaro arrives, carrying a small bottle of honey and a large pitcher of amber-colored drink steeped with ice.

"The honey that these bees produce is very rare and potent," Dante says. "It is potent because it is fermented inside the hive, so it has an alcoholic content."

Lazaro agrees, and starts to dance around. When he stops he passes the honey bottle for everyone to sample.

I savor the ambrosia of underground fermented nectar gathered by nocturnal bees from a night-blooming cactus renowned for its mind-altering spiritual powers. It is a strange mixture of vinegar sour notes, heavy sweet notes of honeydew, and a spicy tanginess like royal jelly. It possesses a distinctive quality of medicinal power and an aura of danger, and I sense that it could easily cause hyperacidity of the stomach and euphoria of the mind.

"This honey is an intoxicant and aphrodisiac," Dante says, stating the obvious. We have all become somewhat flushed and animated. Lazaro begins describing his romantic exploits, as he often does.

"This is a drink that makes people want to dance and make love all night," our teacher goes on. "It can make people drunk, but they wake up refreshed. It is also consumed by men who work hard in the heat, as it gives them energy."

Lazaro pours us tall glasses of ice-cold honey water then returns to his work.

"This species of bee and this honey are unique

to the dry tropical forest, and specifically to where the Palo Santo trees grow," Dante concludes.

We sip the rejuvenating aphrodisiacal intoxicant, reflecting on the mysterious and magical ways of nature and our good fortune to have met this rare medicinal treasure. Outside, the sky has darkened and large drops of rain begin to fall, bringing a breath of coolness through the open windows of the Maestro's indescribably shaped home.

******

There is another tale to be told before the afternoon gives way to blazing displays of evening color, before we light more Palo Santo to ward off the onslaught of mosquitoes, before ending another day well spent in study and dialog, before another farewell to Dante, his workers and family. The Maestro pours us another tall glass of San Pedro mead.

"In the Machalilla Park there used to live many cattle," he continues. "They ate all the Palo Santo seedlings, all the little trees. It was very impressive, the quantity of plants that they consumed.

"For many years the cattle were very dangerous, because they ate the little trees, and those trees could not make seeds. My investigation at the time found that this was a grave problem for the forest.

"I spoke with the Minister of the Environment; he said 'Yeah, yeah, yeah.' I spoke with the community of Aqua Blanca in the park; they said 'What does this stranger want?'

"I was very preoccupied. I sat in front of my fire and prayed to the Palo Santo: 'Please help.'

"Right away came vampire bats. In ten days the vampires killed two hundred cattle in the park, at Los Frailes."

I stare at the Maestro, incredulous. The image of him conjuring a cloud of vampire bats, or invoking the Palo Santo to assist in this way, is stunning. I am also unfamiliar with this species of bat, and not totally convinced that the story is real. Later, I would get confirmation: Desmodus rotundus.

"How did the bats kill the cattle?" I ask, knowing nothing of this local creature.

"They come at night, they put their teeth in, they suck out the blood. Not one, but many. The cow is sleeping, the bats are sucking..."

Dante makes a licking motion showing the

vampires drinking.

"First one, then twenty, then thirty, and finally..."

He mimics a sleeping cow falling over, drained of blood.

"They drink the blood of all animals," he says.

"Humans also?"

"Humans also. Last year there was a problem with the bats attacking people in the Amazon."

He pauses in the story. We reflect on the strange tale he is telling, made more vivid by sipping our mildly hallucinogenic drink. The rain has passed, leaving flowers and leaves dripping in its wake.

"This is very important to understand," Dante says, "because this has a lot of magic."

I nod in agreement.

"The people of Aqua Blanca called the Minister of the Environment. The government sent scientists and veterinarians to investigate what was happening to the cattle. This had never happened before; it was a completely unique event that no one could explain. Maybe it was climate change, as a lot of things are disturbed in the forest. But why in this place at this time, just a few miles down the road in the heart of the Palo Santo forest?"

It was sounding more and more like magic.

"The scientists told the people in the park to put all the cattle into a corral, and to not let them go free."

The Maestro pauses for dramatic effect.

"They told the people that at each of the four corners of the corral they must use smoke of Palo Santo."

It was definitely magic.

"The veterinarians said that Palo Santo smoke is good for keeping away vampire bats."

And all this started because of a prayer to the Palo Santo, I mused.

"The inhabitants of Aqua Blanca came to me and asked for the powder of Palo Santo. They needed much powder to make the smoke effectively, because the wood only burns. I gave it to them as a gift.

"This was good for me, because the cattle were a problem for the Palo Santo. But it was also good for the children, because they need the meat for nourishment. Therefore, it was all good, and I was very grateful."

Dante stands erect, puts his hands together in

prayer, and bows reverently.

"Thank you, Palo Santo."

"You spoke to Palo Santo and asked for help," I said.

"Yes, I asked Palo Santo for help. A short time later the bats came, then the veterinarians came, and then the community came to me asking for Palo Santo."

"And now?"

"Now the cows are not allowed in the park. They are all in corrals."

We laugh from the beauty, absurdity and enchantment of this surreal tale, then raise our glasses of subterranean honey wine in a toast to the power of Palo Santo, to the vampire bats, to the wise veterinarians, to the cows safely protected by the sacred smoke in their corrals, to the young trees that now bear an abundance of seeds, and to Dante, the shaman.

XVI

Medicine For Sadness

The essential oil of Palo Santo is a relatively new botanical product. There are perhaps two or three other distillers of the oil, but Dante is by far the most successful and well known. I do not know if anyone distilled the oil from the wood before he did, but I would be surprised if so. Without a doubt, Dante Bolcato is the primary researcher, innovator, distiller, distributor and educator about Palo Santo oil in the world, and the vast majority of information that is known about it has come from his work.

It is curious to consider that when Dante first met the tree and its fragrance moved his soul and brought him a new life, he had no intention to make a medicinal product. His dream had been to make a perfume, and when he became enchanted by the aroma emanating from the branch that he held on that fateful day in the Machalilla Park, that vision was reawakened. Until now, however, that dream has not been realized, because the medicinal powers and therapeutic benefits of the tree, its wood, its smoke and its essential oil are such a large part of his distillation work, and so closely entwined with the culture and the land, that they have dominated his research.

A day will come soon, I suspect, that Dante's attention will be able to shift from the many responsibilities of being a distiller to fulfilling his desire to create his perfume, a fragrance that captures the complex sweet and spicy notes of the dry forest, the equatorial heat and the beauty of the land. In the meantime, the Maestro is a living encyclopedia of ethno-botanical knowledge about Bursera graveolens; indeed, he is undoubtedly the world's expert on this species, who has not only brought forth years of new research and information, but has gathered and preserved what the local people are rapidly losing of their own traditions. It is Dante, ironically, who has taught the native people of the Machalilla Park much of what they now know of the tree that their ancestors lived with for millennia.

"Tell me about the first time you met the tree in the forest," I ask Dante. We are sitting in his garden on the second day of our visit. "What did you think and feel?"

He reflects back to that day, twelve years ago.

"It was a powerful experience," Dante replies. "I remember having an ancestral connection. I thought 'I have met a very strong medicine that can help people who are sad.' I saw the possibility of being able to offer help, and that this discovery was something important for alleviating sickness."

His comments reminded me of our earliest discussions six years before, when he had given me the first outline of his developing knowledge and experience with the oil. I had taken those simple teachings and shared them with thousands of people, finding that they were indeed valid. Over time, my own studies and research complemented what he had given me, and I was able to slowly elaborate and extrapolate more therapeutic applications, especially when I learned about the extraordinary chemistry the oil possessed.

"When you sent the analysis of the oil I was very moved," Dante says, "because it says it is rich in terpenoids such as limonene. These are compounds that are known in psychiatry for having a strong antidepressant action, and so here is the connection with medicine."

This discovery had confirmed one of the most important uses of the oil that the doctor had previously shared with me. "Inhaling a few drops from the palms has an immediate calmative effect for those who are suffering from the epidemic of urban panic attacks," he had stated. This simple piece of information has reached many people since that day, and in return I have heard many confirmations of its validity.

"Now I am working to produce this essential oil as a medicine for doctors and psychotherapists," he says. He gets up and begins walking back and forth, demonstrating how he uses his walking stick.

"If I am depressed, the psychologist will say 'Take this.'"

He holds up an imaginary bottle of essential oil.

"But what is this? Look at its name: 'Palo' is a stick, a walking stick to hold you up; 'Santo' means a lot of power, because it is divine. In the hands of a doctor, this is very strong medicine."

XVII

The Shaman

There are two things that one first encounters when entering the compound of El Artesan and Dante's home. The first is that just inside the gate you must bend down to pass under an overhanging branch of Palo Santo. The second is that at the top of the path you are greeted by an altar of stone sculptures, crystals and a perpetually burning fire of Palo Santo wood.

I know the significance of the overhanging branch: it is a way to keep alive a custom once widely practiced in daily life by the native people.

Dante has told me several times about this simple but profound ritual: when people left their village and set off on the trail, either into the forest or to another village or town, they would stop at the first Palo Santo tree. They touched it in reverence, and asked it to give protection along their journey. Later, when they returned, they would again greet the tree and offer thanks for a safe return. Now, as Dante would illustrate in his theatrical way, people jump on their motorcycles and race to town, leaving the tree neglected and forgotten.

To enter the world of El Artesan, therefore, you must make the traditional gesture by bowing in order to pass below the tree before you can proceed on your path, and again when you leave. Modern people from the cities need to do this, Dante has explained, to remember their connection to nature.

Up until now the altar and the fire have remained somewhat of a mystery to me. Their positioning and location is striking, being in the central spot where everyone coming and going from all directions must pass. It is not, as one would think, in the most secluded, quiet and private place, but the most active and public. Sara and I have been here at all times of day, yet we have never witnessed it being used for anything in particular, other than the source of a steady stream of fragrant smoke.

Dante has told me about how he spends time meditating with the fire in the altar, and the remarkable story of how he prayed to Palo Santo for assistance when the cows were destroying the trees in the park, but I know nothing about his spiritual practices other than it seems to be a form of homa, the ancient practice of fire ritual. How remarkable that it was such a ritual that first opened the door of synchronistic events that brought me from the beach of Mahabalipuram, only to find it again here.

I am curious about the altar, the fire and what transpires when the Maestro sits with them, but out of respect I am hesitant to start by directly questioning his inner spiritual life. Instead, I inquire about his experiences with local shamans who use Palo Santo, imagining that he has some important and fascinating tales to tell.

"I participated in a ritual with Palo Santo," he tells me. "I met a shaman in Santa Domingo de los Tsachilas; his hair was painted red, his clothes were all made out of feathers."

Dante stands up and walks around the living room, miming as he narrates.

"The ritual is like this. Close the door and the windows so everything is shut tight. Make smoke with Palo Santo, a lot of smoke. The patient is seated there; the shaman is standing here. The patient was a woman who was very sad. She did not know what she wanted. She was crying."

Dante raises his arms, outstretched to the heavens and the four directions.

"The shaman calls 'Listen Pachamama!Help this person! Brother sun, sister moon, mother water!'

"The smoke comes. A lot of smoke is coming.

"The shaman finishes the ritual of talking to the sun and moon and earth. The eyes are stinging. The nose is running. Enough smoke, very strong. The shaman opens the door and says it is finished. The woman, the patient, is happy and smiling.

"I was in this ritual. My eyes were also burning. I thought of only one thing: what is in this smoke? I did not think about the words of the shaman. I thought 'what is in this smoke?'"

We know a few answers from our analysis of the oil: various compounds that are known to have antianxiety and antidepressant effects, working in this case directly on the neurochemistry of the limbic system through the olfactory channels with every inhalation of the smoke. There are undoubtedly compounds other than the aromatic molecules at work as well, and the benefits of prayer. But I am also curious about this obviously psychoactive experience, and will later find intriguing testimonials about the effects of Palo Santo smoke in further research on entheogenic plants and mind-altering substances. Whatever the ingredients, the smoke and oil are, as Dante described repeatedly, powerful healing agents for the mind and emotions, specifically sadness.

The Maestro continues.

"I asked around to meet other shamans of Palo Santo; there was another in the province of Esmeralda. I went to meet him.

"This shaman had long hair, like a Rasta. His house was very dirty. He was dirty. His hands were filthy. His clothes were filthy.

"I said 'Maestro, permit me to know the ritual of Palo Santo.' He said 'If you want to participate in a ritual you must clean the body, the heart, and the clothes with the smoke every day for three months.'"

Dante pauses and savors the moment of irony in his story.

"I am looking at him, and he is very dirty. I said 'Ok, thank you.'"

Dante would never go back, but the shaman's prophesy would come to pass.

"This shaman said 'Go to your house and clean yourself, because you are the man who can bring back Palo Santo and its power."

The Maestro pauses again, and we consider the meaning of the shaman's words, years later. A moment later he speaks again.

"The shaman said 'Palo Santo is powerful, but the people don't know. You are the man that can bring back the life of Palo Santo.' After this he gave me many benedictions. I was grateful for this, and said goodbye and left. I never went back, because I thought he did not want me to come back."

"What else have you learned of Palo Santo rituals?" I continue, hoping to discover something about the fire, altar and column of smoke that perfumes the neighborhood day and night. "What do you do?"

"Every day I wake up at five in the morning. I go down to my altar. There are many things there, very interesting rocks and quartz crystals. There is a large rock in the center, a gift from a Maestro here in

Puerto Lopez who is eighty years old; it is one of the tools of the Indians, for grinding corn."

"I light a fire of Palo Santo. I do this every morning, and in the afternoon at sunset, when the kids are playing with video and my wife is at the Internet, I go and light another fire. I always do it, every day."

I imagine Dante sitting in the translucent colors of equatorial dawn, surrounded by the songs of waking birds, the first stirrings of the village, and the rising smoke from his altar to carry his mind into its contemplations.

"I connect with the positive part of Palo Santo," he says. "I say thank you for the day today. The fire is there, and I think in it. I look at the leaves on the trees; I look at the other things around here. I think about the wood, about reforestation. Time passes, one hour. This hour is very important."

We sit in silence, listening to the sounds of the afternoon. I am appreciative of my teacher's words, but even more, of knowing someone who has the sincerity, discipline and wisdom to return to the elements of nature over and over, with reverence, remembrance and gratitude.

"I have passed my whole life without believing

in a religion," he continues. "I am not a Catholic, I am not a Muslim; no, I am scientific. But now I know what I believe. I believe like the natives, in the Palo Santo. I say 'thank you Palo Santo,' like the natives.

"From doing this, Palo Santo is continually giving me a lot, and the scientific part of me, day by day, is leaving me."

XVIII

The Tree of Life

From the ritual fire on the beach of
Mahabalipuram at the onset of this journey to the
ritual fire in Dante's altar, the story of Palo Santo
has been a series of marvelous synchronistic events.
Dante has many such testimonials as well, the most
dramatic being the sudden appearance of the bats

after sitting at his fireplace and asking Palo Santo for help, or the sudden appearance in his email box of my chemical analysis of his oil immediately after he sent a telepathic message through the smoke asking for that information. Small or large, of greater or lesser significance, these events point to either a mysterious intelligence operating behind or inside the movement of time and space, or simply the magic of coincidence intruding on the mundane world, depending on how one chooses to view them.

There are many parallels between the synchronicity-inducing power of Palo Santo and another species of aromatic tree that I am familiar with. Agarwood has a legendary history of being a "wish-fulfilling gem" as well; it too, through its effects on neurochemistry, somehow alters the flow of time and space in such a way that a chain of spiritual synchronistic phenomena is unlocked. The deep sweet aroma of this wood has long been a part of my life, stretching from my earliest encounters with it during my studies of Asian medicine through meditation retreats infused with its calming aroma during my sojourn at Hsin Tao's monastery. As a result of its presence in my life, many others have come to know and enjoy this pleasantly psychoactive incense, and I have heard enough testimonials of its transformative effects to know that if it is only my subjective imagination, I am not alone.

But synchronicity is only one aspect of positive spiritual magic, a force that expresses itself in a multitude of ways. Both agarwood and Palo Santo are legendary for working in three other ways as well: attracting good fortune, bringing love, and inspiring creativity. Are these four blessings not intimately related? No one can deny that love is good fortune, that love inspires creativity, that creativity can bring good fortune, and that love, creativity and good fortune frequently appear in synchronistic ways.

And so I found myself in the presence of another great tree of mythological power, and saw in Dante's life an example of what I had heard so many times about the mysterious dark resin that forms in the heartwood of Aquilaria agallocha growing in the jungles of Southeast Asia: the power of an arboreal species that offers its life force in the form of a perfumed incense to help people cleanse themselves of negativity and the obstacles it causes, and to support them on their journey to love, happiness, prosperity, inspiration and fulfillment.

******

It is late afternoon when we return to the shady terraces of El Artesan. The heat is gradually giving way to balmy breezes and another spectacular sunset is spreading over the bay. Dante is standing at his fireplace altar; he looks, as he always does, like a man who is fully enjoying his life. He and Rocio have been gone for the day on a trip up the coast to Manta, a beautiful journey they make about once a week to ship El Artesan's products to eagerly waiting customers around the world.

The Maestro greets us warmly, as he always does, and we move up to the veranda where we can look through the green foliage toward the ocean. With classical music and the sounds of children playing in the background, we discuss the topic of the day: love, and the relationship between Palo Santo and good fortune. It is a perfect subject for Valentine's Day.

When we first arrived several days ago I had given the Maestro a gift of agarwood; now I proceed to tell him about its magical powers, so similar to the tree he knows. He listens attentively, and comments on the similarities with Palo Santo.

"I have come to think that Palo Santo is a plant

that helps a person grow," he says. "I believe it has that power because it is 'Santo,' and therefore it is good."

Dante goes on to tell me about an investigation that he is launching, yet another among his numerous projects.

"We are going to do a survey of all the people in the world that distribute the oil we produce. We are going to ask: 'How did it change your life when you met Palo Santo?'"

I agree that this would be an excellent study. The trajectory of his own life, starting with arriving here exhausted and depressed and culminating now in a vibrant life of love, prosperity, happiness and spiritual fulfillment, would be an exemplary case history.

"We have many stories," Dante replies."Many stories of love.

"There is Pedro of Barcelona, forty-five years old. I don't know him; I've never met him, only email. 'Hola, Senor Dante. I need you to provide me with your products, oil, sticks, incense.' After six months, another letter: 'Send me another carton.' Then later he says: 'I am very grateful. It helped resolve a situation with my wife.' Now, after three years he writes: 'Palo Santo is the food, the education, the health of my children and family.' It changed his whole life.

"We have many of these situations. People write and tell me how they have found love and happiness after Palo Santo came into their lives."

He gestures fondly toward the two of us, sitting comfortably with the regal sunset before us.

"And here you are with Sara, newlyweds."

We savor the moment, a moment infused with the essence of what gives life meaning.

"When I first came here I was alone," Dante continues. "It was a dark experience. I had been working so hard for so long, wearing two watches; it was difficult for my mind. Because of this, I want love every day. Every day, when I light the fire in the altar, I want love. I need love."

He points to his heart.

"I, Dante, need love. But Palo Santo also wants love, and it wants to give love. The tree has energy and knowledge that serves people.

"When the natives leave their village they ask for protection for the road. They bow to the tree and tell it they are going to the city. But what do they ask for? They ask the tree to give them love, love to protect them on their journey. When they return, they say 'thank you for the love.'"

Humans need the healing power of trees more than we realize, I reflect. How else can we explain the myriad symptoms of spiritual darkness engulfing the world, other than the absence of love?

Lazaro appears on the balcony, carrying tiny cups of espresso. Along with many other talents he is master brewer, using shade-grown organic Ecuadorian beans alchemically distilled in the espresso maker Dante brought from Italy. I have developed a fondness for this dark elixir, and, unlike other versions I have known that produced unwanted side effects, it seems to have a fondness for me as well.

I remember one of the first things Dante told me about Palo Santo six years ago, as we stood in the open door of his new shop on the gritty malecon in front of the beach. "It opens the channels of creativity," he had said. I had never understood what he meant, exactly. I ask him to elaborate.

"Palo Santo stimulates, generates and produces a lot of creativity," he says.

"How does it do that?" I wonder.

"It is very interesting. Palo Santo helps to

liberate people, to bring out their creative potential. I think the cause is the relationship between the negative energy that it removes, and the space which that creates when that energy leaves."

I consider his words, simple but profound in their meaning, and so aligned with spiritual truth articulated by many wisdom traditions. How could we not become a creatively inspired source of love and good fortune, when our original essence of clarity, brightness and innate joy is liberated from the oppressive weight of opportunistic negativity?

Dante gestures to the workshops of El Artesan, where the day's labors are winding down. Lazaro and Lilliana call from below, announcing their departure. Lilliana may not be returning for some time, depending on when the baby in her womb decides to emerge. The colors of sunset have faded into twilight.

"Lazaro, Lilliana. These are examples of people who were once stones but are now diamonds. Everything everyone does here is art. Look at the beautiful things they are producing.

"Palo Santo gives many people this type of creative work," Dante goes on. "Work is good, and we have to teach people how to make Palo Santo products. This feeds families, and empowers the women, but that is not enough."

The Maestro pauses thoughtfully.

"It is not good when a man beats his wife. Love is something else; it is respect. In the rituals to clean bad energy, Palo Santo helps people with love. We need to teach people how to live the experience of Palo Santo. From that we will see a change in the relationships between men and women. This is the real work, and that is why Dante is a good friend to all the community."

Aromas of dinner are wafting from the kitchen below. The kids are watching Bob Esponja. It is time for Sara and me to consider which version of fish and pasta we will enjoy at the beach.

The Maestro offers some final thoughts.

"Palo Santo is the fragrance of love and life," he says. "It is the aroma of new life, life that comes after death. It is good to use Palo Santo; when we do, we can meet love.

"This morning I went to Rocio and said 'Pardon me, my love. I have something to tell you. For me, today is like every day of the year. Every day is Valentine's Day.'"

XIX

Moon Magic

I am standing in the distillery with Dante, watching a timeless transformation take place, a process that is both simple yet infinitely complex, biochemical yet mystical and metaphorical. Twin blue fires hiss under the two shiny stills, vapor forms into drops that rhythmically roll down the inside of the glass separator into a waiting pool of aromatic water and oil. What is this translucent yellow essence that rises upward to float on the surface of the hydrosol, this fragrant elixir driven by fire and water from its earthly bonds within the steaming wood, only to find itself captured again as liquid gold?

To the extended family that works at El Artesan, it is the gold that becomes the food that feeds their families. To the clinicians and patients around the world who use it for aromatherapy treatment it is a gentle but effective natural medicine. To perfumers it is an intriguing bouquet of fresh citrus and light woody notes. To a researcher seeking new sources of compounds with promise for pharmaceuticals and industry, it is a rich collection of important molecules. To me, it is the sun and moon, earth and rain and wind, the mysterious gravitational field of the equator, and the synchronicity-inducing intelligent life force of a tree that wants to give love and be loved; it is these things to Dante also, which is why we understand each other so well.

The essential oil distilled from the wood of Palo Santo is a new aromatic product, developed and presented to the world through Dante's pioneering work. Like other botanical oils, there are numerous complex and frequently uncontrollable factors that influence the quantity and quality of the final product; likewise, the final product could be described as the expression and culmination of all those factors. On the one hand, the oil reflects

Dante's technical skill and expertise, because there are many complexities and subtleties in the design of the still and condenser units, the temperature, the consistency of the wood powder, and other variables. On the other hand, the oil reflects years of celestial influences and earthly seasons that have been concentrated in the trunk of the tree.

The distillation of essential oils has always been experienced by those with thoughtful minds as both an art and a science that offer glimpses into the diverse fields of chemistry, ecology and botany, a vision which is so intimately linked to the life of the plants that it is difficult to not feel a sense of awe and wonder about the concentrated power that accumulates in the beaker. This sense is heightened when one is confronted by mysteries that cannot be easily explained, such as the effects of the moon on the yield of the oil, or phenomena that seem to contradict the laws of physics and common sense. If nothing else, there is an aura of unseen forces at work that surrounds distillation, which is why it has always been in the realm of alchemical wonder and contemplation.

The distillery is in the same small building that was here when I first met Dante six years ago. Since then, he has expanded the space and added a new still, so he is now working with two. At the time of my first visit I was not able to learn much about the details of his distillation process, other than what he told me about distilling small amounts every day starting on the new moon. Now, I have a much better understanding of the complexities that are involved.

The journey of Palo Santo oil begins in the forest, when the dead trees that have been slowly undergoing their mysterious metamorphosis of resurrection, are finally carried away by Dante's collectors and brought to Alino's woodshed. Under Alino's steady hand the wood is carefully ground into a course powder, which is then taken by Lilliana or Lucio to the distilling room and loaded into the stills.

There are many variables in the wood that influence the quality and quantity of the oil that is distilled from it; the four most important factors are whether it is from a male or a female tree, the region it comes from, how long it has been dead, and how much time has passed since it was removed from the forest.

As Dante explained numerous times, it is the

female trees that produce the most oil, up to twenty times more than males. Their higher concentrations of aromatic compounds can be seen in the coloration of the wood, which is darker than the wood of the males.

Palo Santo wood, like all aromatic plants, also has distinct differences in oil content depending on where the trees grow; these differences are due mostly to ecological influences, such as how far they are located from the coast and the types of soil they grow in. Altitude in particular has a significant effect on the oil content, with the oil content decreasing as the altitude increases. The wood from the Machalilla Park, being at sea level, is therefore some of the highest quality for distillation.

The third factor is the length of time that the tree ages on the ground after it has fallen. Typically, it requires a minimum of three years to mature, with six years being preferable.

The fourth and most intriguing factor is how much time has passed since the tree has been removed from the forest. When the wood is lying in the forest, the oil is increasing in quantity and quality as it ages, but when the wood is moved and brought to the market it begins to lose its essential oil content. Dante describes this by saying that the wood is like a perfume bottle that holds the oil and the forest is the stopper: when the wood is moved from its natural environment it is like taking the stopper off the bottle. What is curious about this is that the same wood, in the same form, can lie on the ground in the forest and increase its oil content, but if that wood is moved it begins to lose its oil content. There is probably a logical scientific explanation for this, but such phenomena are what bring magic to the distiller's art.

Because these diverse factors all go into the still, the oil that finally comes out is an aromatic portrait of Palo Santo's homeland. The wood for distillation arrives from various regions, altitudes and distances from the coast, brought by Dante's team of collectors, and therefore all the forests are represented. There is more than that, however, because Dante also uses the same ratio of male and female wood as is found occurring in the communities of trees: eighty percent female wood and twenty percent male wood.

"For the person who distills but does not know the wood, it is not possible to make a good oil," Dante has said, explaining its complex subtleties.

But the variable elements of the wood are only the first part of the equation; the next part is the still itself, which presents just as many challenges and dynamic factors.

"The still is from Italy," Dante explains. "In Ecuador it costs $12,000. This still is different because the condensing unit comes straight up instead of coming out the side. I don't think this still is necessarily superior, but it is specific and best for Palo Santo."

When filled, the inside of the still is divided into four layers. In the lowest part is a layer of water; above that is a space where the steam rises; above that is a screen; the remainder is filled with the wood powder. Collectively, the lower part with the water and space for steam is about a quarter of the still, and the powder takes up the upper three quarters. There is enough space for the water that even at a high boil it does not touch the wood.

The first step in the distillation process is loading the still. Dante has found that ten kilos of powder is the optimal amount. The powder must be ground to the right consistency; if it is not fine enough, the oil cannot be liberated from the wood by the steam, but if it is too fine the steam will not pass through the powder properly.

Logically, it would seem that the more powder is put in the still the more oil would be extracted. Magically, it does not work that way. As Dante explained, "If you put in ten kilos of Palo Santo you get half a liter of oil. If you put in fifteen kilos, you get half a liter."

Dante described this mystery several times, using examples of other individuals and companies that have tried to extract higher yields, unexplainably without any success.

"I was with a distiller who had a giant still, four meters high, with a huge pipe apparatus. One liter of oil came out. They had big ambitious plans for distillation, but nothing worked out that way."

In response to my scientific skepticism, Dante replied that these results could be easily and repeatedly proven. "It is an incredible thing," he said. "We can do this process many times and you can see my words."

Because there is no obvious scientific explanation for this, it is natural to conclude that the intelligence of the Palo Santo has its own intentions and reasons for such results.

"When I was first learning about Palo Santo, I

talked with it about this problem," Dante said. "Palo Santo does not want a big still, it wants a small still.

"If I have a big still and I can produce five hundred liters myself, it will all be for me. But Palo Santo wants to support many people. Therefore, we need to use small stills. Here, our two stills employ three people who can produce up to one hundred liters a month; if we want two hundred liters, we must have four stills and employ six people. Therefore, the more oil that comes, the more people you will also receive.

"We can see that in this way Palo Santo is a plant that creates equilibrium. No matter how much wood you put in, it will always give you the same amount of oil."

Once the water is added to the bottom of the still and the wood powder is loaded, high heat is given to bring the water to boil. After about an hour steam begins to pass through the condenser pipe and collect as hydrosol and oil in the separator, which are drawn off as they accumulate. When the temperature in the still reaches one hundred degrees Celsius the fire is decreased to a stable boil to maintain that temperature, and distillation proceeds with oil and hydrosol continually accumulating in the beaker.

"Palo Santo is a hot plant from a hot place, and it likes it hot," Dante says. "Therefore, the distillation temperature is very high. You also need a place that is very hot, because the machine needs to be hot on the outside as well." With the two fires going under the stills in a tiny tiled room and the equatorial sun blazing outside, it is indeed a fiery alchemical discipline for those who produce this oil.

Dante points to the cooling system that condenses the steam.

"Here you can see the system for circulating the cold water. The cold water from the cistern below circulates through the condensing coil and then returns back down. It does not consume water, and nothing is wasted."

After about four hours the oil has stopped appearing in the separator. The still is opened, the used powder is removed, fresh powder is reloaded, more water is added, and the process is repeated. In total, about one liter of oil can be distilled from these two runs.

"There is no pressure inside this machine," Dante says in response to my inquiry. "However, there is a return tube here, so the hydrosol recirculates back into the still. This is very interesting because the distilled water has a temperature of ten degrees, and the water inside the still is one hundred degrees. The reaction between them creates a tornado inside the top of the still, which increases the capacity to pull the steam through the wood."

This small tornado inside the still is a very important part of extracting the full range of the oil's aromatic notes.

"During the first part of distillation the oil is a light yellow color and has more top notes of citrus," the Maestro explains. "At the end of the distillation the oil is a yellow gold and has more base notes of wood. The stronger and more profound aromatic notes are stored deeper in the wood, and are the most difficult to bring out. It is necessary to have a machine that pulls them out, and this one permits that."

When the process of distillation is complete, the accumulated oil and hydrosol are poured into a flask for further separation. When that is finished there is nothing more to do but bottle the oil and send it to waiting customers around the world.

But there is one more mystery to ponder.

For some unknown reason, the quality and quantity of oil that is extracted from the wood changes according to the lunar cycle. Specifically, the new moon gives less oil and a lighter aroma, and the full moon more oil and a deeper aroma.

Dante and I spent many hours talking about why this is, trying to come to a reasonable hypothesis.

First, there is no doubt that this is a real phenomenon, because every other distiller of Palo Santo experiences the same thing. It is so noticeable that some distillers simply do not distill on the new moon because the yield of oil is dramatically decreased.

Second, some of the phenomenon is related to the structure of the still, because Dante was able to reduce the large difference between full and new moon yields by making modifications in the condensing unit. But this only answered a part of the question, while raising another: why would the still be structurally susceptible to the moon?

Our inquisitive minds struggled with possible explanations, drawing from what we knew and wondering about all that we didn't. Was there a cellular change in the wood that allowed more oil to come out when the moon was full? We knew that living plants have much more water in them during full moon phases, especially close to the equator where the moon's pull is the most powerful, but could this be the case in a tree that has been dead for years? It was not out of the question, considering the strange process of reincarnation that Palo Santo underwent. Was it simply the power of the moon at the equator, influencing the gravitational fields that affect distillation? It was a good theory, because distillers at other latitudes have not been able to duplicate Dante's high yields of oil, indicating that the moon might be supporting the extraction of the essence from the wood.

Ultimately, we found no satisfying answer. Dante, however, had long ago reconciled himself to the mystery, and had found the obvious solution: distill small amounts of oil on a daily basis starting on the new moon, and blend them all together at the end to represent the entire lunar month. It was a process he had already discovered when I first met him, and one of the first things he taught me about his unique methods of alchemy.

And so the journey of the Palo Santo oil is complete. Within the little bottles that hold the finished product are all the stages and all the influences that contributed to its creation: the death and resurrection of the tree; its location, altitude, ecophysiology, and removal from its forest home; the ratio of female to male wood; the consistency of the powder, the quantity in the still, and intensity of the flame and temperature of the water; the pull of the equatorial gravitational fields; and finally, the waxing and waning of the moon.

"People think it is just a matter of getting the wood and distilling the oil, that it is easy," the Maestro says. "But it is not like this."

Indeed, there is no other distiller of Palo Santo oil who has researched all these diverse factors, and no one who is producing an oil that contains within it the entire complex mixture of elements, energies, terrain and botanical intelligence as Dante, the master distiller, has.

XX

The Alchemist

We are in the distillery, discussing the layers of aromatic notes that present themselves sequentially as the rising steam condenses into the drops that are accumulating in the separator. My attention is drawn to a tarot card in the upper corner of the small room. I remember this card from my previous trip.

"Tell me one thing, please," I ask. "Why Il Diavolo? Is it because it is extremely hot in here?"

Dante smiles.

"It is not only the Devil," he explains. "There is also a mirror."

The card is mounted at the top of a long narrow piece of wood that has a shard of mirror embedded in it.

"The Devil has two angels in front of him. He is seated, like a king. He is the king of the demons."

Dante points to the bottom of the still, where the intense blue flames are fueling the extraction of the Palo Santo oil at one hundred degrees Celsius.

"Here is the fire," he says. "The fire needs to be controlled. To control the fire there is the mirror. The Devil does not want to see himself in the mirror, like a vampire. When a vampire looks in a mirror, it is destroyed. I have a mirror, and with this I can control the Devil."

"And what is the connection between the Devil and the fire?" I ask.

"The fire is necessary to heat the water, therefore we need the Devil. In alchemical language, the Devil is the image of the fire. The woman is the image of the water. The woman with a child is the oil."

Dante goes quiet, and reaches for an empty bottle. He places it under the separator, which is now full of richly aromatic water and a large accumulation of golden yellow oil on the top, and slowly draws off the hydrosol. When he is finished he goes on.

"The child is the oil. It is the union of the masculine..."

He points to Il Diavolo...

"And the water, the feminine..."

He points to the still.

"The fire and the water permit the extraction and separation of the child, the gold, from the dark part, the lead. The work of the alchemist is to transform and separate the darkness to give life. Therefore, the oil is gold. To have the medicine, we need the fire, the man, and the water, the woman."

Dante pauses to wipe the profuse sweat from his face. The distillery is like an oven with the two stills running in the tiny windowless room. Palo Santo likes it hot, my teacher has said many times.

"I can control the fire if it is necessary," the alchemist says.

He reaches up and takes down the board with the card and mirror, and places it at the bottom of the still, facing the fire. His mood is suddenly serious.

"I am the Maestro, not the fire," he says. "I am the Maestro, not the water. I control the elements."

Dante reaches up and hangs the Devil, angels and mirror back in their place. He smiles and leans against the wall, patiently observing the stills as he has done for countless days and nights.

XXI

Medicine

My education about the uses and therapeutic benefits of Palo Santo happened in stages. The first lesson was on the beach in India, where I witnessed the wood being used as an aromatic incense offering. From that alone I could deduce a number of possible benefits, including mood enhancement and the purifying antimicrobial powers that most aromatic plants possessed.

The second thing I learned--when I first went to Ecuador--was that fumigation with smoke from the wood was widely used for repelling the aggressive mosquitoes of the tropics. This further increased my understanding that the tree contained important chemical compounds that probably had a diverse range of important functions.

When I met Dante the first time, he had just started distilling the essential oil of Palo Santo. Prior to that he had spent several years researching the tree's uses in traditional ethnobotanical medicine, and from that could easily extrapolate some of the important uses for the oil. There were two primary things he told me about the therapeutic powers of the oil during that first meeting: that it inspired creativity, and that a few drops could be inhaled directly from the palms to calm panic attacks. This use as an anxiolytic confirmed what I already knew about the psychoactive properties of many aromatic substances that are used in ritual and ceremony.

Between the time that I first met Dante and when I returned six years later, I learned much more about the benefits of this new essential oil that he had introduced to the world, partly through my own research, partly through further correspondences, partly through analysis of the oil, and partly through people's experiences using it. Studying its medicinal and spiritual applications was foremost in my mind when I returned to El Artesan.

******

One of our first discussions was about the early research that Dante had done, inquiring of the native Indians about the ways that they used the wood for healing and ritual.

"There is a market in Machalilla every Sunday where many people come, so it was very easy to do many interviews," Dante said.

"I investigated the medicinal part of Palo Santo, with seven hundred people over one year. I asked two questions: 'Do you know Palo Santo?' and 'What do you use it for?'

"Of the people who were older than forty years, eighty percent knew how to use Palo Santo for medicine, and twenty percent did not know other than for mosquitoes; for those younger than forty years, eighty percent knew it only for mosquitoes and twenty percent for medicine."

"The culture has changed," I commented. It was a story I had heard from every elder herbalist I had spent time with.

"It changed with the arrival of the pharmacy," Dante replied. "There has been a pharmacy in the park now for fifteen or twenty years; the memory of

Palo Santo was very strong before that. The people who go to pharmacies have forgotten how to use it, and the young people don't know.

"But of those who knew its use as medicine, more or less everyone said the same thing: it is good for the respiratory system, joints, urinary system, nerves, and emotional problems.

"My investigations have confirmed that these things are true. It is a medicine that does not require belief. It is like antibiotics, it does not matter if you believe in them or not."

******

Although knowledge of Palo Santo's medicinal uses is fading, there is no doubt that it has been used for healing by the native people for millennia.

"When I first spoke with people in my investigation, I saw that this is a plant that has a very ancient history," the Maestro continues. "There is nothing written, it is only oral history, but truth will walk a long way and a lie will die quickly; I believe this history is a story of the truth, because now we have the studies of scientists and archeologists that have found use of Palo Santo in very ancient cultures.

"We can accept the idea that this tree has been

a part of life of all the pueblos that have been here. Why? Because in this environment there are many, many mosquitoes."

"Yes, they are coming now," I observe. It was time to surround ourselves with the protection of another fragrant cloud of smoke.

"Yes, but there were many more trees in the past, much more nature, many more animals, and so there were even more mosquitoes and they were much stronger. This tree is good for repelling mosquitoes, and vampire bats. I think it is the main plant among all plants that all the people were able to say 'this is medicine.' Therefore, we can easily explain the relationship between Palo Santo and the ancient cultures. It is easy to understand."

"How did the people use the tree in the past that was different than now?" I asked.

"We have one manuscript from the year 1600 that is the most unique document that has been found," Dante answered. "This is from Fraile. He said 'Palo Santo is used as a medicine for all illnesses of a cold nature.' This is the only thing we have."

Dante would make numerous references to Fraile in our discussions, claiming that he was a Spanish botanist who transcribed the words of the native people, recording their lives and knowledge. So far, I have not been able to verify that there was such a person named Fraile. "Fraile," I suspect, is simply what it means in Spanish, which is "friar," and that there were one or more friars who did this work and created these manuscripts.

"Fraile asked the people 'How do you use Palo Santo?' All the people who spoke to him, because there was no pharmacy in 1600, said 'for lungs, for joints.' The philosophy of cold and heat, yin and yang, is ancient. Therefore, for Fraile, an alchemist, it was much easier to just write 'all illnesses of a cold nature,' instead of all the specific symptoms. That is very hermetic, very alchemical.

"And what do the indigenous people say now?" I wondered.

"They say the same thing. They say for the lungs, for the joints; these are cold natured."

"Are there new methods of using Palo Santo that are different from the traditional uses?" I asked.

"Sure," Dante replies. "The oil is new."

He gets up and walks into the house, returning a moment later with a wine bottle full of herbs soaking in alcohol.

"You can put a stick of Palo Santo inside an

alcohol mixture such as this," he explains. He then goes on to name the various ingredients, which include cannabis leaves, and tells how this is a very strong liniment for rheumatism; it is similar to many such formulas that I have encountered in Chinese and Ayurvedic medicine.

"In a nearby town there is a market every day where herbalists sell branches of Palo Santo for tea," he says. "They make mixtures of it with other herbs and give them for various conditions, for the flu, for the lungs. If we go to the market in Puerto Lopez, you can buy the wood, big cartons of it, because the people come to the market to sell it. It is part of the old culture."

******

Part of the research that Dante had done was in the form of large informal trials of the essential oil in the communities of Puerto Lopez and Aqua Blanca in the Machalilla Park.

"Eight years ago, I did an investigation with about 1,500 children," he says. "We have a very big problem here: from the age of three months until the first year, twenty percent of children die from respiratory illnesses.

"I gave the Palo Santo oil to parents, to use on

151

the children. I told them 'Put a drop here on the chest, put it here on the back, put it here on the bottom of the feet.'

And the results, I wondered?

"If you go walking with me in the pueblo you can see that everyone says 'Hola, Don Dante.' These are the parents and their children. From this I have many friends."

This was certainly something that I had seen many times, whenever we were out in public; it seemed that wherever we went Dante was hailed as a highly respected person in the community.

"In another investigation that I did," he goes on, "I gave gifts of fresh oil to many people in the park to use for the children, for asthma, allergies, and other respiratory conditions. Now, the people of Aqua Blanca have knowledge about the medicinal uses of the tree, and they are giving it much more protection."

******

Some of the information about the medicinal powers of Palo Santo that I learned in my discussions with Dante was not related to either its traditional use or the relatively unexplored potential of the essential oil, but to completely unexpected findings.

"This is new information that I have just received," he says.

"On the Isla de la Plata, just off the coast here, there are Palo Santo trees. The guard there is a friend; he has just informed me of something very interesting. There are rats that live on the island, but they are not part of the ecosystem. Therefore, they must put out poison to control them. My friend told me 'Dante, we put out poison for the rats. Later, we observed the rats eating the lower parts of the small trees.'"

The Maestro pauses. We look at each other, already knowing the end of the story and its profound implications.

"Wow," Dante says.

I agree.

"Later, my friend contacted me again. He said 'Dante, the rats ate the poison, then they ate the Palo Santo, and they didn't die. Palo Santo protects the rats from poison.'"

"Impresionante," I reply. I have recently learned this new word and have been waiting for an opportunity to use it.

"This is new information," Dante repeats. "It is

something for us to investigate. However, if we look at the trees, we will see that in the history of their growth, when they were small something ate them, causing a fork in the branches to develop.

"I think that if we investigate, we will find that Palo Santo is a remedy for poisons. If we observe the trees, we can see that at some time in their life something came, maybe cows, maybe other animals, and they ate only this one part, and from that grew two new branches.

"We see a lot of this in the forest, where there are cows, where there are no cows. Maybe it is rats, maybe other animals. Maybe all animals eat it, because there are many plants that are dangerous. Many plants, such as floripondio (datura), are hallucinogenic to animals."

Dante begins to eat an imaginary plant.

"The animal eats a little bit of floripondio..."

He staggers around the room holding his belly and making noises like a hallucinating animal.

"It feels nauseous..."

He grabs an invisible branch and begins munching on it.

"It eats some Palo Santo..."

He stands up straight, feeling better.

"Medicine."

My mind is already exploring the many possible scenarios of what this simple discovery could mean.

"It is something to investigate," Dante concludes. "We have important evidence to start an investigation into whether or not Palo Santo can antidote poisons."

"It is a toxic world," I reply, summing up the potential applications of such a botanical remedy.

******

I knew from my first meeting with Dante that he had been a heavy smoker for many years. I also knew from the analysis of the Palo Santo oil that it was very high in limonene, and from subsequent research learned about the scientific community's interest in limonene as a potential anti-tumor compound. It was therefore extremely interesting to hear about Dante's own personal testimonial about the healing powers of the oil that he had brought to the world, and the implications of what it meant.

"I smoked a lot when I was a psychotherapist, for many years," Dante says. "In 2008, shortly after you were here last time, I was diagnosed with a tumor in my lung. I was terrified. I wanted to go to

Italy for treatment, so I prepared everything, papers, passport, airplane ticket, everything. The plane was leaving in twenty days.

"What did I do? I got a nebulizer. I put three drops of Palo Santo oil in it the first day, six drops the second day, nine drops the third day, twelve drops the fourth day, fifteen drops the fifth day, eighteen drops the sixth day.

"At eighteen drops, after one hour I started coughing. I coughed all night; I thought I was dying. At five in the morning there was one last episode, and then I went to bed and fell asleep.

"At eight in the morning I woke up. My breathing was clear. It was like a miracle. I had so much energy. I was so joyful. It was crazy.

"Two weeks later I went to the doctor and had another scan. The doctor looked at the scan. He looked at it again. He said 'Sir, you should be grateful to God.'

"I said 'thank you very much,' to God and to Palo Santo.

"And here I am, four years later, with strength, and with desire to live. With much more love for Palo Santo, with much more desire to protect and take care of Palo Santo, and to reforest all of it. From this I am very moved to share Palo Santo; it is not only for me, it is for all.

As he has done many times, Dante puts his hands together in a gesture of prayer and gratitude.

"Thank you, thank you, Palo Santo."

XXII

The Aromatic Gem

And so our story ends, in the colors of another equatorial sunset, as we drive down the coast highway. Dante is at the wheel, holding hands and singing Ecuadorian love songs with Rocio; Lazaro, Alejandro, and Kevin are riding in the back of the pickup, Barbara, Sara and I in the back seat. The air is rich with verdant herbaceous fragrances, green islands float in tranquil mirror-like waters offshore. The road winds around broad curves along the cliffs, lined with foliage and fruits of mango, muyuyo, and avocado; passionflower vines drape themselves over fences and poles and shrubs, while the mysterious moonflowers wait patiently to release their inebriating aromas on unsuspecting passersby.

Our destination is The Magic Dolphin, a hidden gem of fine dining in the humble pueblo of Salango, a few miles south of Puerto Lopez. Around a few more corners waits a rendezvous with plates of aphrodisiacal barnacles, dishes of fine ceviche, grilled corvina served with plantains and a bottle of Spanish wine; the boys will feast on chips and orange Fanta, and Dante will let Rocio drive us home.

It has been a memorable adventure, worthy of celebration.

Physically, it was intense and demanding, with unmistakable manifestations of what traditional Chinese medicine would describe as "damp heat," including a plethora of redness, itching and swelling from the aggressive and ubiquitous mosquitoes waiting just out of Palo Santo's reach; abdominal pain, diarrhea and fever from monsoon-nourished microbes in the food; sinus inflammation from the toxic dust of the streets; and humid lethargy only temporarily alleviated by another cold shower, another nap under the fan, and another shot of espresso.

But these were minor irritations, in

comparison to the pleasures.

Intellectually, it was a feast of rich stories and studies, delicacies to nourish the mind.

Emotionally, it was a journey through a fragrant landscape where around each corner waited another joy: friendship, laughter, discovery, and revelation.

Spiritually, it was an immersion in the matrix of creativity, a baptism in the womb of inspiration, a vision of a sacred dimension of healing, good fortune, art, poetry, and the blessings of natural prosperity unveiled by the purifying smoke and illuminated by the golden elixir produced by Palo Santo's mysterious process of resurrection.

This morning is an excellent example. We arrived early, and found everything quiet and peaceful before another day of work and activity. I wanted to finalize details with Dante concerning some items we were taking home as mementos of our time with him: a piece of Palo Santo wood and an incense burner. He had mentioned that he had a piece of wood picked out, but I had yet to see it.

The maestro was walking down the path toward us as we entered, and offered his usual enthusiastic greeting. At my inquiry, he led us into the workshop, and pulled out a gnarled piece of wood, about three feet long.

This is no ordinary piece of wood, he said, but a treasure of such antiquity that it has become petrified, fossilized.

He held it up for me to examine where he had cut one end. It was polished and burnished, its ring patterns of growth glowing with shades of golds and browns and yellows and earth tones.

"It is a gem," I commented, struck by the fact that the years had transformed it from plant to stone.

"Yes, it is a gem," he replied. "But it is aromatic."

Dante offered the polished end, and I marveled that a piece of petrified wood could emit such an exquisite aroma.

"How much is something like this worth?" I asked, my curiosity overcoming my knowledge that such talk degraded the meaning of the gift.

"These pieces are now incredibly rare," Dante replied."In the last three years I have found only this one. It is priceless."

He held it out to me.

"You cannot buy this. It is something that can

only be given, from one shaman to another."

I accepted his gift: it looked like finely carved wood, was heavy and hard like stone, and had a perfumed aura.

How does one convey the nobility of such an action by a teacher, earned or unearned on my part? How can one describe the incomparable dignity, wonder, wholeness and satisfaction of such a moment? How does one describe the unique spiritual power stored in the last precious remnants of nature's once abundant treasure house of magical objects? Perhaps in words of forgotten languages, words whose utterance arose from a more ancient, uncontaminated human mind, a mind whose wisdom knew the meaning and value of such things.

XXIII

Un Abrazo

It is already hot at eight in the morning when we arrive for the last time at Dante's sanctuary. We drop off some household items we no longer need, discuss last minute details about the road ahead, have a final espresso and then bid farewell to everyone. Dante accompanies us to the gate; our driver, Fernando, is waiting to transport us through landscapes of coastal forests, steaming malarial marshlands, rich agricultural plateaus, and then up the towering western flank of the Andes into Quito's cool valleys.

"I never say goodbye without an embrace," the Maestro says. We embrace, and in that moment I see and feel all the things that I have come to know about my teacher, and more.

He is the alchemist and master distiller, who learned his art and science not by studying with others, but by vigilant days and nights in the tiny room with the fire of the still, listening to the sound of the water and steam and wood and oil as they underwent their mysterious transformations, observing the influences of the moon, tides and equator in the drops of golden elixir slowly accumulating in the beaker.

He is the ethnobotanist who gathered the disappearing remnants of what the elders knew and remembered about the arboreal treasure in their forest, preserving and propagating this knowledge for the world as the younger generation forgot.

He is the botanist and environmentalist who was the first to unlock the secret of germinating Palo

Santo, the caretaker of thousands of seedlings, the one who has overseen the replanting of tens of thousands of trees, and the man whose vision, mission, message and life purpose is to create immense forests.

He is the entrepreneur and businessman who transformed a local ecological resource into a sustainable enterprise that has brought prosperity to his growing extended family, and with it empowerment for those burdened by the weight of oppressive cultural history.

He is the healer who freely offered the medicine of his Palo Santo oil to local families, in the process saving the lives of hundreds if not thousands of children who otherwise would have perished in the epidemic of infant mortality caused by preventable and easily treated conditions.

He is the teacher, storyteller, comedian, shaman and mystic, who lights a fire of Palo Santo wood every morning at dawn and every evening when work is done, who sits gazing into its smoke and sending blessings from his heart to all who might be inhaling its sweet fragrance.

He is Don Dante, a respected elder, community leader, father and husband.

All this was there, in the moment of that embrace, and something else. Would there not be, in the heart of a man like this, a tenderness and vulnerability born of years of sacrifice, now repaid many times over with love?

It must have been, for I thought I saw a tear in his eye when we finally turned away and drove off.

Epilogue

On Mar 15, 2012, at 7:12 PM, Dante Bolcato wrote:

Rocio just gave me great news, that I will be a father again, and I tremble like the strings of a violin. Today, our hearts want to share with you the arrival of our next child, because it is when you and Sara were here that he began his journey.

Today I also got the ingredients for the perfume: pepper from Santo Domingo de los Tsachilas, very spicy and very tasty, leaves and flowers of guayavana, and cinnamon from the Amazon rainforest.

Un abrazo, Dante

www.elartesan.com.ec

The Journey Continues...

Watch exclusive video footage from David Crow's journey to Ecuador to visit and study with the mysterious alchemist Dante Bolcato. The video includes footage of Dante, tours of the exotic locales described in the book, and David's commentary on Sacred Smoke and his 'palo santo journey'.

These bonus digital materials are included with this book, and add a vivid dimension to the magic and mystery of Sacred Smoke.

For free and immediate access, visit the following website:

www.floracopeia.com/sacredsmoke

About the Author:

David Crow is the author of "*In Search of the Medicine Buddha*," a book about his ethnobotanical studies of Tibetan and Ayurvedic medicine in the Himalayas. He is an acupuncturist and herbalist with over thirty years of clinical experience in traditional Chinese and Ayurvedic medicine, and the founder of Floracopeia, a company that supports ecologically sustainable agriculture through the production of essential oils. Mr. Crow is the cofounder of The Learning Garden, one of the country's largest school gardens, that has helped bring cultivation of organic food and medicinal plants into the Los Angeles public school system.

To learn more about David Crow, Floracopeia, and Palo Santo products, visit **www.floracopeia.com**

About the photographer:

Sara Crow is an acupuncturist and herbalist with a Master's degree in Traditional Chinese Medicine. She specializes in using Flower Essences and is the creator of Floracopeia's FlorAlchemy products. Sara is a nature photographer with a unique gift for photographing flowers.

Also by David Crow:

In Search of the Medicine Buddha

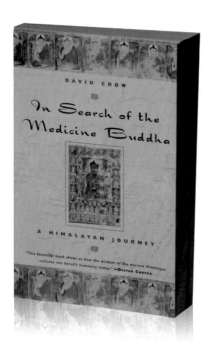

A colorful and captivating story of adventure, exploration, and self discovery, In Search of the Medicine Buddha transports readers into the life and work of David Crow and his teachers of medicine. It is a journey into the wonders of Himalayan herbology and spirituality, written in lyrical prose that interweaves valuable medical teachings with insights into the

Buddhist and Hindu cultures of Nepal. Appealing to those interested in exotic places and genuine mystical encounters, this account of one man's search for authentic lineages of Himalayan medicine evokes the beauty and wonder of a faraway land, and reveals a hidden world of powerful and increasingly important healing knowledge.

"David Crow's vision of enlisting the healing plants in the effort to heal the the environment is an excellent insight, really illuminating, and beautiful as well. He writes beautifully and he has a solid knowledge of the plant kingdom and its role in salvaging our health from its currently predicament. David makes the ancient teachings of Ayurveda, Chinese medicine, and Tibetan medicine relevant to our times, without compromising his respect and reverence for the traditions. I absolutely loved it. So did everyone else I gave a copy to."
Robert Thurman

"This beautiful book shows us how the wisdom of the ancient Himalayan cultures can benefit humanity today."
Deepak Chopra, M.D.
Author of "How to Know God"

"David Crow provides great insights into the healing practices of Tibetan medicine and Buddhism. This book is a wonderful integration of spirituality and medicine."

Dr. Vasant Lad
Author of "Ayuveda: The Science of Self-Healing"

"A fantastic read! This is a contemporary account of one man's journey into the past to learn the ancient secrets of healing. David Crow's book delves deep into the roots of ancient herbal medicine."

Michael Tierra, L.Ac.
Author of "Planetary Herbology"

"As Indian and Tibetan medicine become popular in the West they, like yoga and meditation, are too often stripped of their rich cultural context. David Crow was fortunate to have met outstanding physicians in his travels, and made the most of his fortune by dedicatedly absorbing what they offered him. His fascinating account of apprenticeship and discovery opens a wide window for the reader into the laboratory of true healing art."

Dr. Robert Svoboda
Author of "Ayurveda: Life, Health, and Longevity"